LIFEQUEST™

BY DORA B. MAYS, Ph.D

TRILOGY

PROFESSIONAL PUBLISHING MEETS POWERFUL PROMOTION

A wholly owned subsidiary of **TBN**

LifeQuest™

Trilogy Christian Publishers A Wholly Owned Subsidiary of Trinity Broadcasting Network

2442 Michelle Drive Tustin, CA 92780

Manufactured in the United States of America

10 9 8 7 6 5 4 3 2 1

Library of Congress Cataloging-in-Publication Data is available.

ISBN: 978-1-63769-348-3

E-ISBN: 978-1-63769-349-0

ACKNOWLEDGMENTS

To the many women and men in my personal and professional life who have been my beta test for the content of *LifeQuest™,* allowing me to walk you through the content, information, and exercises to discover its validity and effectiveness. Your enthusiastic reception and gracious confirmations of praise and demand for more have encouraged and affirmed me in this assignment. Thank you for your willingness to take this journey with me and for trusting where I took you. You did not just trust the process; you trusted me in the process. Mere words are insufficient to fully relay my appreciation, so I have put these words right here at the beginning of this completed work in hopes that you will see them and know that I will never forget you, and what was sown in me has taken root and produced a harvest of bountiful proportions. It is my desire that this book is seedlings that will be planted in the lives of so many others and will continue to produce fruit in lives for generations to come.

TABLE OF CONTENTS

FOUNDATIONAL SCRIPTURE

"For I know the plans I have for you," says the Lord. "They are plans for good and not for disaster, to give you a future and a hope. In those days when you pray, I will listen. If you look for me wholeheartedly, you will find me. I will be found by you," says the Lord. "I will end your captivity and restore your fortunes. I will gather you out of the nations where I sent you and will bring you home again to your own land."

Jeremiah 29:11-14 (NLT)

PREFACE

Proclamation

I will approach LifeQuest™ with an open mind.

I will consider the possibility of a new perspective.

I will admit that my way so far has not worked.

I will commit to the reading and completion of the discovery tasks.

I will be open to letting go of the past and embracing the future.

I will make changes by changing my words, then my mind, then my beliefs, and, ultimately, my behavior.

I acknowledge that the only thing I control is *me*.

I will navigate and embrace the journey!

Affirmation

"You can't go back and change the beginning, but you can start where you are and change the ending."

C. S. Lewis

Scripture

"Commit your work to the Lord, and your plans will be established."

Proverbs 16:3 (ESV)

Prayer

I have accepted the opportunity and made the decision to take this journey called LifeQuest™. I open my ears, my mind, and my heart to hear from you, Lord, to conceive your instructions and convictions. As you impart your Word to me in this process, I am willing to consider my ways and yours. I am willing to endure the process of circumcision for the benefit of transformation. I acknowledge that my way has only gotten me this far, but your way will take me all the way. I am ready for the journey with you as my guide. Amen.

Objectives

- To learn the basis and process for LifeQuest,™ the testimony that inspired it, and the divine order of progression through the journey.
- To establish individual expectations and commit to the exercises and activities that will assist with your personal LifeQuest™ experience.

TESTIMONY

Dora—a Survivor's Story

It was mid-December 2001 in Tampa, Florida, when I received my last round of chemotherapy just days before, and its brutal effects had long since taken ahold of me. Because we were at the end of this routine, my husband Michael knew my schedule like clockwork. Expecting it to be several more hours before I should awake from my drug-induced sleep, he decided to take a quick trip to his office at MacDill Air Force Base. He was a Senior Non-Commissioned Officer (SNCO) in the Air Force, still on active duty at that time, and needed to deal with a situation that required his attention. Up until this day, Michael had been by my side continually; at every hospital visit, every chemotherapy treatment, every blood draw—continually! Between him and my mother, I was never alone.

On that infamous day in December, Michael had no reason to think that I would awaken any earlier than normal and believed he would return long before. But there was nothing normal about that day. It was a day of reckoning, the day the spiritual battle for my life was waged in my body. All of a sudden, I was awakened violently from my sleep, calling on the name of Jesus. I was undeniably aware of the fight for my life that was occurring within me.

I was also resigned that to continue lying in bed sleeping could result in my eternal slumber. The cancer was gone, but the very potent drugs that had been administered to eradicate the disease created a path of destruction almost as deadly as the disease itself. I knew I had to get myself out of bed in order to not succumb to death. With every possible ounce of strength in me, I made my way to the floor, crawled to the bathroom, and willed myself to get into the shower. Once there, almost in a panic, I questioned my decision. How could I manage to bathe, exit the shower, dry, and clothe myself when all of my energy had been expended just getting to the shower? But somehow, I did just that!

After a brief pause to summon new strength, I used the support of the garden tub and vanity to pull myself to a vertical position. Then for the first time in weeks, I found myself standing in front of my full-walled mirror over the vanity in my bathroom with an unobstructed view of the physical effects of cancer and the chemotherapy used to eliminate it. The shock at what I saw floored me. But before I actually fell, a flood of thoughts raced through my mind; "Who is that?" "Is that me? It has to be me because there is no one else here." "Wow!" "Oh, my God…it is me!…, and I am so…" but before I could covert my thoughts into words, my eyes became blind, and I could no longer see the reflection that was once before my eyes. My mouth was under arrest, and I also could not speak the words that had come to mind. In dark silence, I was my own observation. My memories were rewound and playing on fast forward. I remembered having cancer, having surgery to remove the cancer and my entire right breast, areola, nipple, plus more than twenty-something lymph nodes with it. I also remembered the eight-hour sessions of chemotherapy over two consecutive days, every twenty-one days in a cycle. I recalled the havoc it reaped on my body, barely allowing me to have any appetite at all and rejecting most of what I managed to get down. I did not forget the rush of what was appropriately called the "Red Devil" (Adriamycin) running through my veins and destroying every cell in its path, both good and bad, making my hair a casualty of the war. As I recollected myself and regained some semblance of control over my thoughts, it all began to make sense.

It had to be me reflected in the mirror I faced. Although I remembered each of the links in the chain of events, I had not had an occasion to see them all connected together. This was the first time. Like a personal portrait on a canvas, the memories reflected the scar where one breast had already been removed, and the anticipated loss of the other appeared almost evident. No hair and the revelation that a person's face looks totally different without eyebrows and lashes. Before me stood in full view an image of the frame of my body totally reshaped by the loss of weight and loss of anatomy.

The culmination of realities, visually, mentally, and physically before me, was too powerful to process. In a blink, with the brightest of light blinding my eyes, my thoughts arrested, my mouth and thoughts silenced by alarm, and unable to speak, I collapsed to the floor with my mind focused on the flaws and visual deficiencies. While I lay prostrate on the floor of my bathroom in disbelief, my awareness was miraculously changed from the physical to the spiritual. I could hear the sweetest voice begin to speak to me. I was reassured that I am not the flesh that I saw or that was missing, but rather I am the internal light that blinded my eyes and inhibited me from continuing to see the physical reflection that caused my alarm. At that moment, I was forever changed. My vision and perspective about who I am was shifted beyond my exterior self to the greater person on the inside. I was familiar with the voice that was speaking to me. It was not my own, but one just as familiar to me. I had heard it many times before. It was the voice of God speaking; my own thoughts were focused on the carnal flesh and not the spiritual self. I heard him say that "I am His Spirit residing in an 'earth suit' that allows me to function in this space and time. He told me that I should *not* focus on the suit because it is just material substance and insignificant to the overall mission for which I was designed to achieve. He explained that the body is just the container, and although it is needed to carry me through life on this earth, it is the content that is most relevant. He reminded me that I had been commissioned to deliver that message to others, but I had to understand and accept it myself first. He instructed me to go in search of the understanding of who I am and to know without a doubt that I am who I am because of Him and my decision to give my life to Him. He has taken up residence in my body and made it possible for me to carry the mission to the world.

Once I regained full consciousness, I was energized enough to finish my grooming, dress, and return to my bedroom, where I sat in my recliner and began to read my Bible. While reading, I discovered a note that I had written in 1999. The note had five references for self, and my writing included notes about my personal vision in each of these five areas (Spiritual, Social, Mental, Physical, and Financial). I had written goals in each of the areas and a projected date to achieve them. Obviously, I had written the note with some thoughtful consideration and then tucked it away in my Bible for safekeeping with no further reference, accountability, or plan for the accomplishment of those goals. At that moment, I was convicted! How could I have obeyed God in writing the vision (Habakkuk 2:2-3) but stopped short of seeing it through? In my state of conviction, I vowed to reevaluate the goals I had written, establish a plan, and appropriate actions to accomplish them. At that moment, I was the first participant of LifeQuest™. As I committed to finish what God had started with me in 1999, He began to reveal His divine order for the process. As I continued to obey, He continued to give me the next step and the next. I resolved my personal LifeQuest™ and graduated with my Doctor of Philosophy degree in 2008 (one goal of my Mental Quest). I am finally following the lead of the Holy Spirit, as an act of obedience, and writing this amazing AMaysing Quest for Life. Should you choose to take this journey, you will discover or clarify your divine purpose and establish a plan to accomplish it— LifeQuest™!

INTRODUCTION

LifeQuest™ is a divinely inspired process for considering all aspects of life with the objective of exploring and discovering purpose and meaning. It is a journey through decisions, life events, and circumstances in search of peace. The process of LifeQuest™ is personal. The coordinates for getting to the place of peace require awareness of where you have been, where you are now, and the direction of your progress. The quest should begin in a season of life when you are ready to be honest and open to self-awareness, deep internal personal and interpersonal introspection, and willingness to *let go* and *let God*! If you choose to believe that God not only knows but established the plans for your life and desires for those plans to be fulfilled, how are you positioning yourself to have the plans made known to you?

LifeQuest has three mazes called "quests." There is a divine order to LifeQuest™. Maze one is *Relational* and has three quests; (1) *Spirtual*, (2) *Sexual*, and (3) *Social*. Maze two is *Transitional* and has two quests; (4) *Emotional* and (5) *Mental*. Maze three is *Continual* and has the final two quests; (6) *Physical* and (7) *Financial*. There are seven total quests to process. Each quest will be explained in greater detail as we progress. LifeQuest™ is a *journey*, not a *destination!*

The journey begins with Relationships. You must first work through the Spiritual and the relationship with God before you can progress to the Sexual, which transverses through milestones to understand the relationship with yourself first and then with an intimate partner. Until you have a healthy relationship with yourself, you are not ready to have the ultimate intimate relationship with another person. Perhaps you were wondering why your marriage did not work, or how you keep choosing one unhealthy relationship after another, or why you can't seem to connect with a mate on a deeper level. I once heard someone say, "A healthy you is essential for a healthy relationship." One definition for *relationship* is "the way in which two or more concepts, objects, or people are connected or the state of being connected." The Holy Spirit separated the word and revealed the meaning to me in this way, "*re*—regarding, *late*—after the expected time, *tion*—the condition of being, *ship*—a large vessel for transporting people." In other words, a relationship should be regarded as the most significant means of transporting people into the condition of *being* over a period of time, not your time—His Time! He went on to clarify that we are missing the most vital aspect of life because we do not understand our role in the "relationships" that we are a part of. He established relationships as the primary vessel for transporting His people

22

in life, and we are missing the expected time for connecting for a number of reasons—like two ships passing in the night, unaware of the existence of the other or worst, with no regard or respect for the other.

We were created to be in relationships with others. We were not meant to be alone. Remember God said, "It is not good that the man should be alone; I will make him a helper suitable for him" (Genesis 2:18, NIV). God even directed animals in pairs to enter the ark to be spared from the flood that would destroy the earth (Genesis 7:15, NIV). The third and final relational quest is *Social.* This quest explores all other relationships, especially parent/child, and siblings. These relationships are particularly challenging because they are the ones you inherit rather than choose. Our relational person is continually evolving (becoming), a work in progress that is intended to shape us in ways that connect us with others as we travel this life journey.

For this reason, relationships must be the first mile of the journey. I do not profess to know all there is to know about relationships. However, I am *compelled* to share what I have learned. Relationships can teach us some valuable lessons about life, and I continue to learn them every day that I live. Understanding my role in relationships has been a continual work in progress. A point of clarity came for me when trying to help my oldest daughter understand this truth.

As a mother, I have made many parenting errors. I am blessed that the grace of God has covered my daughters despite my shortcomings. When I was a teenager growing up under my parents' authority, I recall being told that I could not have a boyfriend until I was sixteen years old. I am not sure what made sixteen the magic age, but since it was what my parents permitted, I figured it was the "right" age, and in my mind, it became the standard for my daughters. In theory, it was fine, but I never stopped to consider that my daughters were not the same people that I was as a teen. They were not growing up in the same era or experiencing the same things in their lives that I had in mine. By the time my oldest daughter became sixteen years old, I had begun my own personal journey in LifeQuest™ and was in a thriving spiritual relationship. During my prayer time and inquiry about my daughter dating, I was certain that she was not ready. I believe the Spirit of God impressed upon me that she needed to have a relationship with Him first and then herself before trying a romantic relationship with a young man. Equally significant of a lesson, she needed to understand her role in her relationships before she would be ready for an intimate relationship with another person.

At first, I was not clear what that meant, so The Holy Spirit referred me to her relationship with her younger sister. He reminded me that in her relationship with her sister, she was the oldest but still uncommitted to doing what she knew was "right," regardless of whether her younger sister did the "right" thing or not. Instead, she had the audacity to act as though her behavior was justified because her younger sister had done something "wrong" first. This was a very difficult but valuable lesson for her and me on the importance of having a healthy relationship with self before a relationship with others. I knew that my daughter's embarkation with dating would have to be delayed, but convincing her of that would be a battle beyond my expectation. It became a battle of wills. This lesson is one that would have to be learned one way or another. The necessity will become more relevant during the *Sexual* Quest.

The *Spiritual Quest is* a journey through the most primary and significant relationship, the one that establishes the basis for all others. It is both *vertical* and *eternal*, with the *Most High,* your Creator. Second is *Sexual*, a two-fold quest; personally with yourself, then with your significant other. Both parts are *internal* and *intimate.* The last of the relational quests is *Social.* It consists of the milestone that includes all other relationships; parents, children, siblings, friends, co-workers, neighbors, etc. It includes all *horizontal* and *external* relationships. They may also be intimate and include people with whom you share lifetime connections.

The *Transitional Quests* are the *Emotional* and *Mental Quests*. The *Emotional Quest* is the bridge in the journey. Before you are able to ascend the bridge and cross over into your purpose, you will need to shed any emotional baggage that may hinder your progress. Once the emotional dispositions have been settled in your life, you are ready for the next phase of the journey, the *Mental Quest*. It requires thoughtful reflections. You will be encouraged to start "thinking about" *what* you are "thinking about." It is a point of decision—*purpose* and *meaning*. It requires academic and vocational considerations. You will be challenged to answer the questions, "What do you know or what do you need to know in order to do and be what God has called you to do and to be?"

The final milestones in the journey are where maintenance occurs, the Physical and Financial Quests. The Physical Quest is personal responsibility and for maintaining a temple that is fit for service. It is not necessarily about physical attributes that tend to shift our focus to vain considerations; however, those obstacles will also have to be considered and addressed during this quest. Habits, choices, and decisions that demonstrate self-regulation will be explored. The Financial Quest is about accountability and stewardship. It is the place for determining your personal accountability for all of the gifts, talents, and treasures that have been entrusted to you. You will be challenged to also consider whether you have been a responsible steward over them. Your accountability is not to man or self only, but ultimately to God!

Welcome to the journey!

REFLECTION

I am reminded of a story in the Old Testament about an Israelite woman who was about to give birth when she heard that the Ark of the Covenant that housed God's presence had been stolen. She was so upset by this that she named her newborn boy, Ichabod, meaning, "The glory has departed." This woman put her focus on what was happening in her present situation and allowed her present to dictate her future. She could have just as easily named her son something that meant, "The glory will return," but she was so focused on the negative, so caught up in where she was at the moment that she defined her future by her present state. Don't be like this woman. I employ you to learn from this woman, don't ever determine your future based on your present. You may have had some difficult times in the past, and your current state may not look very promising. The truth is that your future should be declared in faith (confidence in what we hope for and assurance about what we do not see (Hebrews 11:1, NIV).

The first and most primal relationship you will encounter is a parental relationship. In the natural sense, it is a relationship between a mother and her child at birth. While that relationship is extremely important and not to be discounted, it is not the first relationship that must be considered in your journey through life. The first parental relationship has to be the one between you and your Father. Not your earthly father; your heavenly. The one who created you, the giver of life. The one who established your purpose and equipped you to fulfill it. In order to truly consider anything of importance about your life and purpose, you must first settle the question; to whom do you give credit for your life and existence. The decision is individual, personal, and necessary to know in order to continue. It has to be answered by you, for you.

Your belief system was likely established by a parent or the cultural society where you grew up and matured. We typically subscribe to the beliefs of the person(s) of influence in our life. For the purpose of LifeQuest, it is not enough to just believe what others have taught or suggested you believe. You will need to determine for yourself what you believe and why you believe it. It will need to be based on your self-proclaimed reference for truth and the one you believe to be the sustainer of your life. It must be deeply internal and personal, eternal and the source of your hope, for it will be your guiding principle—the navigator for your journey.

As I shared with you in my testimony, my point of reckoning came when I realized that my faith and what I believed could no longer be about what my mother or father told me was true and right. In the face of my morbidity and mortality, it had to be about what I knew for myself was true. In the wake of death, would what I believed provide me hope and assurance or leave me doubting, questioning, or in disbelief? It was certainly personal and necessary for the place I found myself at that moment in time and the days that followed. So it must also be for you.

PLAN OF SALVATION

I would be remiss if I continued this instruction without allowing an opportunity for you to consider your eternal life. While continuing this journey does not require that you accept or establish a relationship with Jesus Christ, the basis for its content is based on scriptural references from the Holy Scriptures that are inspired by Him. The premise of the philosophical framework is based on faith and personal acceptance of salvation. For this reason, I am compelled to offer you the plan of salvation.

Since I am a visual person, I offer this common picture of salvation as a reference for your understanding of what it means to accept the free gift of salvation.

Mankind was separated from God by a large pit called *"sin."* The only way to reach God was through an appropriate connection that would bridge the gap, cover the pit of sin, and make it possible for us to get across to Him.

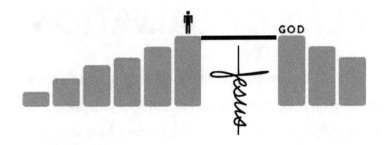

That bridge was *Jesus*.

Separation from God is the result of sin and sinful behavior. Romans 3:23 states, "for ALL have sinned and fallen short of the glory of God." "We all, like sheep, have gone astray, each of us has turned to his own way; and the Lord has laid on Him the iniquity of us all" (Isaiah 53:6, NIV).

Sin must be punished. The eventual punishment is eternal separation from God—hell. Romans 6:23 (NIV) states, "For the wages of sin is death, but the gift of God is eternal life in Christ Jesus our Lord." In order to gain a relationship with God, salvation is required. It is not earned, but given through grace as stated in Ephesians 2:8-9 (NIV), "For it is by grace you have been saved, through faith—and not from yourselves, it is the gift of God—not by works, so that no one can boast." Titus 3:5 (NIV) also states, "He saved us not because of righteous things we had done, but because of His mercy. He saved us through the washing of, rebirth and renewal of the Holy Spirit." "All of us have become like one who is unclean, and all our righteous acts are like filthy rags; we all shrivel up like a leaf, and like the wind our sins sweep us away" (Isaiah 64:6, NIV).

From the beginning, God had a plan for you to have a personal relationship with Him. The way was through the death of His son, Jesus Christ, the only perfect redemptive sacrifice. His love for us was demonstrated by his death while we were still in the midst of our sin (Romans 5:8). He loves you so much that He was willing to sacrifice His son, Jesus, to pay the price for your salvation (John 3:16). The only thing you have to do is confess that "Jesus is Lord" and believe in your heart that His death and resurrection were payment for your life and salvation (Romans 10:9-10). The process is as easy as A-B-C, Admitting/Accepting, Believing, and Confessing.

PRAYER OF SALVATION

Jesus, I did not deserve it, but I know that you died for me. I am a sinner that is separated from you because of my sin. I repent of my sins and choose a life in relationship with you. I accept the life that you paid for with yours and will spend the rest of my life living according to your will and your way. I accept your plan for my life and will strive to fulfill your intended purpose. Please come into my life and live through me. Amen.

Your personal repentance of sin and acceptance of Jesus Christ for the forgiveness and redemption of sin assures you a relationship with Him and grants you entrance into eternal life—heaven (see John 1:12; John 3:36; Luke 15:7,10). This plan will ensure your salvation and access to the gift of eternal life in Christ (see 1 John 5:13; John 5:24).

Accepting Jesus Christ as Lord and Savior of your life is to also accept that in creating you and establishing your purpose, He equipped you to fulfill it. Spiritual gifts are an indication of God's call and purpose for your life (see Romans 12:2-8). Everyone has a specific gift(s) for the fulfillment of his/her call (see 1 Corinthians 7:7). Every *Christian* has at least one spiritual gift (see 1 Peter 4:10), and no one has all of the gifts (see 1 Corinthians 12:28-30). Spiritual gifts are for the common good to build up the Body of Christ (see 1 Corinthians 12:27).

SECTION ONE

THE RELATIONAL QUESTS

Affirmation

"The purpose of life is a life of purpose."

Robert Burns, Scottish poet

Scripture

"And this is the testimony; God has given us eternal life, and this life is in his son. Whoever has the Son has life; whoever does not have the Son of God does not have life."

John 5:11-12 (NIV)

The relational quests consist of the Spiritual, Sexual, and Social. The journey has to begin with relationships because God is a relational being. He does not just exist as a figment of our imagination. He is a being and, as such, expects to have a personal relationship with us. He desires to be accepted and connected. Like any relationship, it requires constant contact and continual effort.

As previously stated, you must begin with the Spiritual Quest. It is the most primal of all of our relationships and sets the tone for every other interaction. Once you are clear about your relationship and connection to the Most High—God, you will be capable of having a relationship with yourself and others; *not until*!

The two parts of the Sexual Quest; relationship with self, then relationship with another, intimately. If you are clear about your significance to God and His unconditional *love* for you, it will be possible for you to love yourself and to give and receive love from another. Without this assurance, self-love can become self-loathe or some other perversion of love. Without it, love for others and from others can become idolatry or some other unhealthy expression. It is vitally important that you understand how to love from the one that is *love* so that you have a proper perspective of *love* and understand your role in a loving relationship.

Finally, the Social Quest completes the relational quests and guides you through the process of horizontal relationships with every other person in your life, both family and friends. The interesting consideration about relationships with family is that the only person that we are related to (family) and that we are able to choose (besides adoptions) is the person we marry. In some cultures, you don't even get to choose the person you marry. Therefore your relatives are people that result from someone else's decisions but impact your life and existence. Your parents are people who came together to conceive you, and not every conception occurs in the context of love and affection. Your siblings are also someone else's decision, as are your aunts, uncles, cousins, etc. It is left to you to determine how you relate to these relatives. We will get into more considerations during the Social Quest.

PROCLAMATION

Lord, I am reminded of the story of Jesus in the garden of Gethsemane and His fervent prayer that you would not require His life and suffering as the ransom for all mankind. I realize that He was committed to ministry and serving people, but when it came to the ultimate sacrifice and the pain and suffering that He knew it would take to accomplish your will, He briefly wavered and requested an out. As I become aware of your call for my life and the possible sacrifices and discomforts that may be required in order for your will to be accomplished, I want to decline! I can think of so many other ways, so many other people who I believe could and would do it instead of me. Help me to continue to consider the reference you have given me in Christ, although uncomfortable, help me to be willing to surrender my will for yours and declare, "nevertheless, not my will, but yours be done" as He did. Help me to "be strong and courageous, not afraid *or* terrified, for you Lord are with me; you will *never leave* nor *forsake* me" (Deuteronomy 31:6, NIV). As I embark on this journey called LifeQuest™, I will be open to relate to you and others in my life. I will accept my role in those relationships and will commit to do as you instruct me in pursuit of the life you have promised me. I thank you for your sacrifice of life for me to have mine. I will not let your death be in vain. I am here, Lord, guide me to my *purpose!*

SPIRITUAL QUEST

Affirmation

"Our relationship must be right with God before it can be right with man."

Billy Graham

Scripture

"I will guide you along the best pathway for your life. I will advise you and watch over you."

Psalm 32:8 (NLT)

Prayer

Lord, as I embark on this journey, be my guide. Provide clarity about my spiritual beliefs and practices. If I am in error in any way, please redirect me. Show yourself to me and help my unbelief. This journey is personal and significant to me. I need to know who you are so that I can understand who I am and who I am to be in this life so that I will know my role in all other relationships. Show me the good, the bad, and the ugliness in my life, and in my awareness, give me the courage and means to make the changes that will put me on the path that you have mapped out for my life. You gave me this life; now show me how you intend for me to live it. I want to learn the things you are teaching me so that I can make the right decisions for life on this earth and eternally. Amen.

Objectives

- To determine your personal belief system and spiritually connect with purpose and meaning in your life.
- To understand your role and the role of the Most High in your spiritual relationship.
- To establish trust within the relationship that will cause you to *always* consult with God for direction in your life; to acknowledge Him in *all* your ways (Proverbs 3:6, NKJV).

A *vertical* and *eternal* relationship

The Spiritual Quest is a unilateral, one-on-one relationship between you and the creator, God. The relationship is vertical because of the hierarchy of God, being a higher being than you. It is *eternal* because of the necessity of the relationship being one that is never-ending so that it may govern your life and every other relationship in your life. It has to be the primal relationship that establishes the basis for all others and the prerequisite for your life's journey.

The Spiritual Quest establishes the primary and most essential relationship, the one between you and the creator, the Most High God as your Lord and Savior. This relationship is both vertical and eternal. It is where the foundation of life begins and ends. Without this very primal relationship, we simply exist. The acknowledgment and connection with a being greater than yourself is the essence of life and must be settled personally in order to have meaning and purpose. Spiritual confirmation through a personal relationship is the catalysis for LifeQuest™!

This is not a reference for a particular religious practice. It is about a philosophy for life that connects you with a power greater than you. It is through a relational connection that instruction and guidance for your life will happen. Without it, aimless wandering and uncertainly or self-propelled travel through life will lead to a sequence of wrong turns, dead-ends, and detours in the journey.

It is the one-on-one personal relationship with your God. It is defining who He is to you and how He speaks to you. It is the certainty of His voice and His character, as to not confuse Him with your own fleshly desires and thoughts and to not mistake Him for the sinful influence of Satan or others. It is establishing Him as the *first and foremost* relationship in your life and the director of your journey. It is the decision to follow, not lead. It is getting to an understanding of *whose* you are so that you can ultimately discover *who* you are!

Consider your one-on-one relationship with your God. Think about the communication, transparency, trust, and affirmation of that relationship. In order for you to relate to anything or anyone in life, you must first come to know how to relate to God, the creator of all things and humankind. It is He who has made us and therefore established the life He expects for us. Speaking from my personal spiritual perspective, I identify my God as Jesus Christ. If you choose to accept the life He has paid for with his *blood* for you, a relationship is necessary.

The relationship with Him will provide clarity about your life, past, present, and future. It is through Him that you will come to realize the hindrances to your accomplishments and the necessity of the trials that you will or have already experienced. It is through Him that your divine purpose will be revealed and fulfilled. The relationship will reveal who He is to you, how He speaks to you, and clarify His voice and character, distinguishing it from your own thoughts, misdirected, or even sinful influence of Satan or others.

I should pause here to address the possible discontent with repeated male references for God. Perhaps you struggle with that gender reference for your own reasons. I would ask that you keep reading. Regardless of your issues with male authority or with God being referred to as a male, as the giver of life, the truth is that even in the natural, males carry the seed of life, without which life will not be. This in no way minimizes the female and her significance to life-giving. She holds the egg in her womb, and without it, the seed is just a seed and could not produce life.

You may be placing human expectations on God based on your experiences with other humans. These parameters may inhibit your ability to trust Him or your willingness to follow Him. When you think about where you are in your relationship with God compared to where you know you should be, what is the reason for not being where you should be? Consider the comparisons you make about God because of his *man*hood that either help or hinder your ability to trust, obey, and follow His lead in your life.

As a *father*, He is the protector and provider. If you

have not had a father who has protected and/or provided for you, it may be a struggle to allow God to establish your reference. May you need to overcome your current reference before you trust Him as your Father? If your father was never there or abandoned you, or if he should have cared for you, but instead, he hurt you physically, emotionally, mentally, or even sexually, it would be understandably difficult to accept God as your Father, especially since He is not physically present. Although He manifested on this earth as a man, fully human (see Hebrews 2:17, NIV), "He is not a man, that He should lie..." (Numbers 23:19, NKJV).

There are many reasons why it may be difficult for you to see God as your Father. What are your reasons?

_____

_____

_____

_____

_____

_____

_____

_____

What about the person of Jesus Christ as your *Lord* and *Savior*? Is there a reference in your life for a controlling or manipulating man who treated you as a possession instead of a person to love and respect? Or perhaps there were no significant men in your life, and all of your references are of women. It may be difficult for you to imagine a man being your Lord and Savior if you have only had great women making the difference for you. Are you able to love, honor, and respect Jesus and trust His plan for you, allowing Him to chart the course for the journey of life?

Although I have never had a brother, I reference Christ as my big brother. For me, that reference means someone who looks after me and ensures that no one or nothing harms or hurts me. He comes to my rescue when I am in trouble or danger and sticks up for me. He fights my battles and is always willing to put His life on the line for mine; He is my brother, who always protects, always defends, and always covers me. He sacrificed His life, paid the price, and carries me.

What about the person of the *Holy Spirit*? He promised to be our *comforter*. If the last man you trusted, betrayed you or hurt you, or the one you gave your heart to broke it and left you wounded, or you have always been the one taking care of the men in your life, not the other way around, why would you trust or surrender control of your life to another man with promises? Well, again, He is not like any of those men. His promises are true, and He never breaks them. However, you will have to be willing to surrender and allow Him to fulfill His promises to you. It will be necessary for you to let down the walls and barriers that you have erected to shield yourself from the anticipated hurt you have come to expect, therefore keeping Him at a distance and unable to comfort, console and care for you? You have rejected Him and the wisdom that comes through Him because you doubt and deny that He would love you enough to want the best for you and ensure that you have it. If any of this sounds familiar, take time to reflect and consider making a change.

List the men in your life and put a (+) beside the ones that have provided a positive reference for you and a (-) beside the ones that were less than positive.

_____

_____

_____

_____

_____

_____

_____

This is a place of decision for you. "*God* is *not* a *man* that He should lie, neither the son of a man that He should repent…" (Numbers 23:19, NKJV). *God* is *God!* He is three in one, *Father, Son,* and *Holy Spirit.* He should not be held to the same standards as *man.* This is a good time for you to decide to *trust him* with the life He has given you. After all, "He came that you can have an abundant life" (John 10:10b). You can choose to blame God for failed relationships with men in your life and remain estranged from Him, or you can place the blame where it belongs with those men for the decisions they made or yourself for the decisions you made. It is your choice, what will you choose?

It is a relationship. No, it is *the relationship*! Relationship with God through Christ is the epitome of *love.* If you have never tried it, make the decision to try this relationship today (refer to the Plan for Salvation mentioned previously). If you have tried it but lost your way because you compared it to another human relationship that fell short of your expectations, repent and give it another try. It will empower you to *live.* I'm not talking about being religious. Religion dictates what you should do or not do but does not empower you to do it. I am talking about having a relationship. It is only through relationship that you will acquire the essentials for achieving your divine purpose in life. The relationship makes the difference.

When you decide to trust God and to consult with Him about the direction of your life, you will realize His purpose for your life. The foundational scripture for LifeQuest™, Jeremiah 29:11-14, speaks about the plan that God has for your life. He has a role in the process, but so do you. He is willing to reveal His plan and empower you to fulfill it if you are willing to seek Him for instruction and obey what He tells you to do. "To obey is better than to sacrifice... rebellion is as the sin of witchcraft and stubbornness is as iniquity and idolatry" (1 Samuel 15: 22-23, NKJV).

God declares, "I will guide you along the best pathway for your life. I will advise you and watch over you" (Psalm 32:8, NLV). If you accept that as truth, allow Him to demonstrate His love toward you by seeking Him for instruction and counsel. It is His role to instruct you and teach you about His plan for your life. His goal is for you to succeed! Why would He have a plan for you and not reveal it to you or do what He can to ensure it is carried out? It makes no sense for Him to have a plan and not relay it to you in a way that you understand and can comply with. He's your Father, and someone once said, "Father knows best!"

He knew you when He created and established your purpose; therefore, He also knows that you have the capacity to contain your purpose and to fulfill it. He only needs you to believe and receive the truth that He already knows. Faith is required because you may not be able to see with your natural eyes the result of your fulfilled purpose. You may have difficulty accepting that God would choose to use you to fulfill the call. Doubt may be more evident, making it easier to deny the truth than to accept it. Faith is required! *Faith* is *not* a *feeling;* it is a *fact.* Until now, you may have been depending on your own senses, what you can see, touch, hear, and think. But as it is written, "Eye has not seen, nor ear heard, nor have entered into the heart of man, the things which God has prepared for those who love him" (1 Corinthians 2:9, NKJV). Through the loving relationship with God, and only through that relationship will God reveal what He has prepared for you.

DISCOVERY

In preparation for His divine call and purpose for your life, God has blessed each believer with Spiritual Gifts. Do you know what spiritual gifts God has given you? Here is one version by LifeWay Christian Resources for your reference (printed by permission of LifeWay Christian Resources). This Spiritual Gifts Survey will help you determine what spiritual gift(s) and/or special talent(s) God has specifically entrusted in you.

SPIRITUAL GIFTS SURVEY

Directions

This is not a test, so there are no wrong answers. The Spiritual Gifts Survey consists of eighty statements. Some items reflect concrete actions; other items are descriptive traits, and still, others are statements of belief.

- Select the one response you feel best characterizes yourself and place that number in the blank provided. Record your answer in the blank beside each item.

- Do not spend too much time on any one item. Remember, it is not a test. Usually, your immediate response is best.
- Please give an answer for each item. Do not skip any items.
- Do not ask others how they are answering or how they think you should answer.
- Work at your own pace.

Your response choices are:

5-Highly characteristic of me/definitely true for me.

4-Most of the time, this would describe me/be true for me.

3-Frequently characteristic of me/true for me—about 50 percent of the time.

2-Occasionally characteristic of me/true for me–about / 25 percent of the time.

1- Not at all characteristic of me/definitely untrue for me.

_____ 1. I have the ability to organize ideas, resources, time, and people effectively.

_____ 2. I am willing to study and prepare for the task of teaching.

_____ 3. I am able to relate the truths of God to specific situations.

_____ 4. I have a God-given ability to help others grow in their faith.

_____ 5. I possess a special ability to communicate the truth of salvation.

_____ 6. I have the ability to make critical decisions when necessary.

_____ 7. I am sensitive to the hurts of people.

_____ 8. I experience joy in meeting needs through sharing possessions.

_____ 9. I enjoy studying.

_____ 10. I have delivered God's message of warning and judgment.

_____ 11. I am able to sense the true motivation of persons and movements.

_____ 12. I have a special ability to trust God in difficult situations.

_____ 13. I have a strong desire to contribute to the establishment of new churches.

_____ 14. I take action to meet physical and practical

needs rather than merely talking about or planning to help.

_____ 15. I enjoy entertaining guests in my home.

_____ 16. I can adapt my guidance to fit the maturity of those working with me.

_____ 17. I can delegate and assign meaningful work.

_____ 18. I have the ability and desire to teach.

_____ 19. I am usually able to analyze a situation correctly.

_____ 20. I have a natural tendency to encourage others.

_____ 21. I am willing to take the initiative in helping other Christians grow in their faith.

_____ 22. I have an acute awareness of the emotions of other people, such as loneliness, pain, fear, and anger.

_____ 23. I am a cheerful giver.

_____ 24. I spend time digging into facts.

_____ 25. I feel that I have a message from God to deliver to others.

_____ 26. I can recognize when a person is genuine/honest.

_____ 27. I am a person of vision (a clear mental portrait

of a preferable future given by God). I am able to communicate vision in such a way that others commit to making the vision a reality.

_____ 28. I am willing to yield to God's will rather than question and waver.

_____ 29. I would like to be more active in getting the gospel to people in other lands.

_____ 30. It makes me happy to do things for people in need.

_____ 31. I am successful in getting a group to do its work joyfully.

_____ 32. I am able to make strangers feel at ease.

_____ 33. I have the ability to plan learning approaches.

_____ 34. I can identify those who need encouragement.

_____ 35. I have trained Christians to be more obedient disciples of Christ.

_____ 36. I am willing to do whatever it takes to see others come to Christ.

_____ 37. I am attracted to people who are hurting.

_____ 38. I am a generous giver.

_____ 39. I am able to discover new truths.

_____ 40. I have spiritual insights from Scripture concerning issues and people that compel me to speak out.

_____ 41. I can sense when a person is acting in accord with God's will.

_____ 42. I can trust in God even when things look dark.

_____ 43. I can determine where God wants a group to go and help it get there.

_____ 44. I have a strong desire to take the gospel to places where it has never been heard.

_____ 45. I enjoy reaching out to new people in my church and community.

_____ 46. I am sensitive to the needs of people.

_____ 47. I have been able to make effective and efficient plans for accomplishing the goals of a group.

_____ 48. I often am consulted when fellow Christians are struggling to make difficult decisions.

_____ 49. I think about how I can comfort and encourage

others in my congregation.

_____ 50. I am able to give spiritual direction to others.

_____ 51. I am able to present the gospel to lost persons

in such a way that they accept the Lord and

His salvation.

_____ 52. I possess an unusual capacity to understand

the feelings of those in distress.

_____ 53. I have a strong sense of stewardship based on

the recognition that God owns all things.

_____ 54. I have delivered to other people's messages

that have come directly from God.

_____ 55. I can sense when a person is acting under

God's leadership.

_____ 56. I try to be in God's will continually and be avail

able for His use.

_____ 57. I feel that I should take the gospel to people

who have different beliefs from me.

_____ 58. I have an acute awareness of the physical

needs of others.

_____ 59. I am skilled in setting forth positive and precise

steps of action.

_____ 60. I like to meet visitors at church and make them feel welcome.

_____ 61. I explain Scripture in such a way that others understand it.

_____ 62. I can usually see spiritual solutions to problems.

_____ 63. I welcome opportunities to help people who need comfort, consolation, encouragement, and counseling.

_____ 64. I feel at ease in sharing Christ with nonbelievers.

_____ 65. I can influence others to perform to their highest God-given potential.

_____ 66. I recognize the signs of stress and distress in others.

_____ 67. I desire to give generously and unpretentiously to worthwhile projects and ministries.

_____ 68. I can organize facts into meaningful r elationships.

_____ 69. God gives me messages to deliver to His people.

_____ 70. I am able to sense whether people are being honest when they tell of their religious experiences.

_____ 71. I enjoy presenting the gospel to persons of other cultures and backgrounds.

_____ 72. I enjoy doing little things that help people.

_____ 73. I can give a clear, uncomplicated presentation.

_____ 74. I have been able to apply biblical truth to the specific needs of my church.

_____ 75. God has used me to encourage others to live Christ-like lives.

_____ 76. I have sensed the need to help other people become more effective in their ministries.

_____ 77. I like to talk about Jesus to those who do not know Him.

_____ 78. I have the ability to make strangers feel comfortable in my home.

_____ 79. I have a wide range of study resources and know how to secure information.

_____ 80. I feel assured that a situation will change for the glory of God even when the situation seems impossible.

LEADERSHIP

Item 6 + Item 16 + Item 27 + Item 43 + Item 65 = TOTAL

_____ _____ _____ _____ _____ _____

ADMINISTRATION

Item 1 + Item 17 + Item 31 + Item 47 + Item 59 = TOTAL

_____ _____ _____ _____ _____ _____

TEACHING

Item 2 + Item 18 + Item 33 + Item 61 + Item 73 = TOTAL

_____ _____ _____ _____ _____ _____

KNOWLEDGE

Item 9 + Item 24 + Item 39 + Item 68 + Item 79 = TOTAL

_____ _____ _____ _____ _____ _____

WISDOM

Item 3 + Item 19 + Item 48 + Item 62 + Item 74 = TOTAL

_____ _____ _____ _____ _____ _____

PROPHECY

Item 10 + Item 25 + Item 40 + Item 54 + Item 69 = TOTAL

_____ _____ _____ _____ _____ _____

DISCERNMENT

Item 11 + Item 26 + Item 41 + Item 55 + Item 70 = TOTAL

_____ _____ _____ _____ _____ _____

EXHORTATION

Item 20 + Item 34 + Item 49 + Item 63 + Item 75 = TOTAL

_____ _____ _____ _____ _____ _____

SHEPHERDING

Item 4 + Item 21 + Item 35 + Item 50 + Item 76 = TOTAL

_____ _____ _____ _____ _____ _____

FAITH

Item 12 + Item 28 + Item 42 + Item 56 + Item 80 = TOTAL

_____ _____ _____ _____ _____ _____

EVANGELISM

Item 5 + Item 36 + Item 51 + Item 64 + Item 77 = TOTAL

_____ _____ _____ _____ _____ _____

APOSTLESHIP

Item 13 + Item 29 + Item 44 + Item 57 + Item 71 = TOTAL

_____ _____ _____ _____ _____ _____

SERVICE/HELP

Item 14 + Item 30 + Item 46 + Item 58 + Item 72 = TOTAL

_____ _____ _____ _____ _____ _____

MERCY

Item 7 + Item 22 + Item 37 + Item 52 + Item 66 = TOTAL

_____ _____ _____ _____ _____ _____

GIVING

Item 8 + Item 23 + Item 38 + Item 53 + Item 67 = TOTAL

_____ _____ _____ _____ _____ _____

HOSPITALITY

Item 15 + Item 32 + Item 45 + Item 60 + Item 78 = TOTAL

_____ _____ _____ _____ _____ _____

Now that you have completed the survey, thoughtfully answer the following questions.

The gifts I have begun to discover in my life are (Record your top three Spiritual Gifts):

1. _____

_____

2. _____

_____

3. _____

_____

Are any of these gifts a revelation or a confirmation for you? If so, Which ones and why?

_____

_____

Are you currently using any of these Spiritual Gifts? If so, how? If not, why?

_____

_____

_____

_____

_____

_____

Complete the following statement, after prayer and worship; I am beginning to sense that God wants me to use my spiritual gifts to serve Christ's body by:

_____

_____

_____

_____

_____

_____

If you are not sure, make the following confession: I am not sure how God wants me to use my gifts to serve others, but I am committed to prayer and worship, seeking wisdom and opportunities to use the gifts that I have received from God. Ask God to help you to know how He has gifted you for service and how you can begin to use these gifts to minister to others.

These references may provide some perspective about your purpose. There are many different gifts; to serve, speak, write, and it is the Spirit of God who gives the gift.

| ADMINISTRATION (SERVING) | 1 Corinthians 12:28-31 Luke 14:28-30 | A divine enablement to understand what makes an organization function and the special ability to plan and execute procedures that accomplish the goals of the ministry. |

| GIVING (SERVING) | Romans 12:6-8, 2 Corinthians 8:2-5; 9:6-15, Mark 12:41-44, Matthew 6:3-4 | A divine enablement to contribute money and resources to the work of the Lord with cheerfulness and liberality. |

| HELPS/HOSPITALITY (SERVING) | 1 Cor. 12:28-31, Ro.12:6-8; 12:9-13; 16:1-2, Acts 9:36; 16:14-15, Mark 15:40-41, Gal. 6:2, 1 Pet. 4:9-11, Phil. 2:19-23, Luke 10:38; 22:24-27, John 13:14; Heb. 13:1-2 | A divine enablement to care for people by providing fellowship, food, and shelter; working gladly behind the scenes in order that God's work is fulfilled. |

| INTERCESSION (SERVING) | Ephesians 6:18, 1 Timothy 2:1-2, 1 Kings 13:6, Luke 11:1-10, Matthews 6:6-15, Mark 11:22-25, James 5:14-16, Colossians 4:12-13, 1 Thessalonians 3:10 | A divine enablement to consistently pray on behalf of and for others, seeing frequent results. |

| LEADERSHIP (SERVING) | Romans 12: 6-8, Hebrews 13:7; 17 | A divine enablement to bring truth to cast vision, motivate, and direct people to harmoniously accomplish the purposes of God. |

| MERCY/ COMPASSION (SERVING) | Romans 12:6-8, Luke 7:12-15, 10:30-37, Matthew 5:7; 20:29-34; 25:34-40, Mark 9:41 | The divine enablement to cheerfully and practically help those who are suffering or are in need by putting compassion into action. |

FAITH	1 Corinthians 12:28-31, Mark 16:17-18, Acts 8:13; 9:36-42; 19:11-12; 20: 9-12, Hebrews 2:4, Romans 15:17-19	A divine enablement to be firmly persuaded of God's power and promises to accomplish His will and purpose and to display such a confidence in Him and His word that circumstances do not shake that conviction.
MUSIC	1 Samuel 16:14-23, 2 Samuel 6:14-15; 1 Corinthians 14:26, Psalm 96;1-2; 100:1-2; 149:3; 150:1-6, Colossians 3:16, 2 Chronicles 5:2-13	A divine enablement and capability to present personal witness and inspiration to others through instrument, singing, or dancing.
WRITING	1 John 2:1; 2:12-14, Luke 1:1-3, 1 Timothy 3:14-15, Jude 1:3	A divine enablement to express truth in a written form; a form that can edify, instruct, and strengthen the community of believers.
DISCERNMENT	1 Corinthians 12:7-11, 1 John 4:1-6, 2 Chronicles 2:9-16, Psalms 119:125, Proverbs 3:21, 1 Kings 3:9, Hebrews 5:14	A divine enablement to distinguish between truth and error, to discern the spirits, differentiating between good and evil, right and wrong.
TEACHING	Ephesians 4:11-16 Romans 12:6-8 1 Corinthians 12:28-31 Hebrews 5:12-14 Acts 18:24-28	A divine enablement to understand, clearly explain, and apply the word of God causing greater Christ-likeness in the lives of listeners.
PROPHECY	1 Corinthians 12:7-11; 12:28-31; 14:1-5; 14:24-25; 14:30-33; 14:37-40, Romans 12:6-8, Ephesians 4:11-13, Deuteronomy 18:18-22	A divine enablement to reveal truth and proclaim it in a timely and relevant manner for understanding, correction, repentance, or edification. There may be immediate or future implications.

APOSTLE	1 Corinthians 12:28-31, 2 Corinthians 12:12, Ephesians 4:11-16, Matthew 10:1-8, Acts 2:42-44	A divine/spiritual appointment to exercise general leadership or oversight over a number of churches with God-given authority and proclamation to teach the true doctrine.
EVANGELIST	Ephesians 4:11-16, Matthew 28:16-20, Acts 2:36-40; 8:5-6; 8:26-40; 14:21, 2 Timothy 4:5	A divine enablement to effectively communicate the gospel to unbelievers so they respond in faith and move toward discipleship.
PASTOR (SHEPHERDING)	John 10:1-16, Acts 20:28, Ephesians 4:11-15, 1 Timothy;4:11-16; 3:1-7, 2 Timothy 4:1-2, 1 Peter 5:1-4	A divine enablement to nurture, care for, and guide people toward on-going spiritual maturity and becoming like Christ.
HEALING (SIGNS)	1 Corinthians 12:7-11; 12:28-31 Acts 3:1-10; 14:8-10, James 5:14-16, Luke 9:1-2	A divine enablement to be God's means for restoring people to wholeness (physically, emotionally, mentally, or spiritually).
MIRACLES (SIGNS)	1 Corinthians 12:7-11; 12:28-31, Mark 16:17-18, Acts 8:13; 9:36-42; 19:11-12; 20:9-12 Hebrews 2:4, Romans 15:17-19	A divine enablement to serve as a human intermediary through whom He performs acts of supernatural power that are recognized by others to have altered the ordinary course of nature and authenticated the divine commission.
MISSIONARY (LEADERSHIP)	Ephesians 3:6-8, Mark 16:15, Acts 1:8; 13:2-5; 22:21, Romans 10:14-15 1 Corinthians 9:19-23	A divine enablement to minister whatever other spiritual gifts they have in another culture. A stronger-than-average desire to be a part of the fulfillment of the Great Commission around the world.

"TRUTH OR DARE"

Tell the truth or dare to live with the consequences. Journal your truthful awareness about your divine purpose; what has God been prompting your heart about, but you have denied or refused due to fear, sacrifice, or other reservations?

_____

_____

_____

_____

_____

_____

_____

_____

Have you ever had any special inclination to be or do anything in particular?

_____

_____

_____

_____

_____

_____

_____

Has anyone ever spoken "prophetically" over you about a call or purpose for your life?

_____

_____

_____

_____

_____

_____

_____

Are there certain things or certain groups of people that appeal to you, or you believe you are drawn to them? If so, make note of those promptings, inclinations, prophecies, and/or things/groups of people, i.e., teens, elderly, men/ women, children.

_____

_____

_____

_____

_____

_____

_____

_____

_____

_____

_____

_____

_____

_____

_____

Reflection

Who do you seek for guidance in your life? Why?

_____

_____

_____

_____

_____

_____

Were you taught to subscribe to a specific belief system by your parent(s) or the adult(s) who influenced you in your formative years? If not, where have you acquired your beliefs?

_____

_____

_____

_____

_____

_____

_____

Do you continue to subscribe to those beliefs?

_____

_____

_____

_____

_____

_____

_____

Have you challenged those beliefs to determine if they are "just" your parents/caretaker's beliefs or embraced them as your own? What is your resolve?

_____

_____

_____

_____

_____

_____

_____

"I will instruct you and teach you in the way you should go; I will counsel you with my loving eye on you" (Psalm 32:8, NIV). What comfort does this biblical reference give you about God's plan for your life as opposed to your plans or the plans of others?

_____

_____

_____

_____

_____

_____

"After he has gathered his own flock, he walks ahead of them, and they follow him because they know his voice" (John 10:4, NIV).

Notice that the shepherd walks ahead of his sheep, gently calling them to follow. What change do you need to make in your life so that you can look for God's hand at work and listen for His voice alone?

_____

_____

_____

_____

"If anyone would come after me, let him deny himself and take up his cross daily and follow me" (Luke 9:23, ESV). When you consider following God's plan for your life, what do you think you will have to deny in order to follow Him?

_____

_____

_____

_____

_____

_____

"I pray also that the eyes of your heart may be enlightened in order that you may know the hope to which he has called you, the riches of his glorious inheritance in the saints, and his incomparably great power for us who believe" (Ephesians 1:18-19). The sight of our heart is "*faith*"…believing and having hope in what is not actually seen. What do you believe in faith about the "call" or "purpose" for your life?

_____

_____

_____

_____

Faith is the confidence that what we hope for will actually happen; "And it is impossible to please God without faith. Anyone who wants to come to him must believe that God exists and that he rewards those who sincerely seek him" (Hebrews 11: 6).

Proclamation

I accept that my spiritual relationship with God is personal, and the decision is mine to choose Him. He already chose me. I choose Him as my Lord and Savior, discarding all negative references from my life experience with men that have failed me. I surrender the references and wounds caused by those relationships to God, and I believe that He will vindicate me and restore *all* that I lost in the process. I choose to *trust*, I choose to *follow*, I choose to *obey*, I choose *life!*

SEXUAL QUEST PART ONE

Relationship With Self

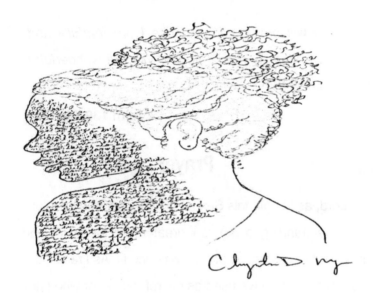

Affirmation

"This above all: To thine own self be true, and it must follow, as the night the day, thou canst not then be false to any man."

William Shakespeare

Scriptures

"God created man in His own image, in the image of God He created him; male and female He created them."

Genesis 1:26-27 (KJV)

"I will praise you because I am fearfully and wonderfully made; your works are wonderful; I know that full well."

Psalm 139:14 (NIV)

Prayer

Lord, as I begin this Sexual Quest, open the eyes of my understanding to see your greater plan for my life and how the circumstances of my existence fit. As I recall, the messages that I have used as my reference for who I am, help me to sort them and only keep the ones that agree with what you want me to know about *me*. Reveal every detail of my perspective and adjust it to fit *your* truth. I want to know and to be the person you created me to be. I want to trade the lies that I have accepted for your truth, and the bitter sorrow for blessed assurance manifested as *joy*. Amen.

Objectives

- Review the *Discovery* exercises from the previous section and note the outcomes.
- To become more self-aware, understanding who you are, and accepting the person that God has created you to be.
- To become more mindful of the influences of your personal past and present experiences and how they impact your future, assessing the sources of your perspective in order to discard the lies, accept the truth, and embrace the essence of you.
- To discover your role in the relationship with yourself first and then become prepared to give the truth of yourself to a deserving intimate partner in preparation for an exclusive long-term commitment and marriage.

The Sexual Quest is first an internal process of discovering who you are on your way to becoming who you will be—dealing with the good, the bad, the ugly, and the naked truth about your choices and experiences (decidedly and uncontrollably yours). It is a personal journey through the messages, references, and experiences in your life that you have agreed with and assigned to your identity.

The journey will require you to assess the messages and, in some cases, change or rescript them in order for you to see yourself through the eyes of God, your creator. He declared, "You will know the truth, and the truth will set you free" (John 8:32, NIV). It is time to come out of the closet, to take off the mask or the veil that has disguised your true self. No more pretending to be someone you were never meant to be. No more cop-outs or blaming others for who you are or are not. No more making excuses for not being the person God created you to be. The first part of the Sexual Quest will explore the person you are physically, mentally, emotionally, and spiritually. Ann Landers stated that "The naked truth is better than a dressed-up lie." It is a point of decision to be the "*student* of *you*" first so that you can be the "*teacher* of *you*" when required.

DISCOVERY

Personality Assessment

Search online to find a simple personality assessment that will give you some insight into your personality type. Most of them are compartmentalized into four types. From as far back as 400 BC, when Hippocrates philosophized that most people fit into one of four temperaments: Sanguine, Melancholic, Phlegmatic, and Choleric. By the 1920s, along came Psychologist Carl Jung with his four personality types: sensor, thinker, feeler, and planner. Then more recently, Isabel Myers and Katherine Briggs expanded the philosophy to include distinctions between introvert and extrovert, resulting in the Myers Briggs Type Indicator (MBTI). Having eight personality outcomes instead of four: introvert, extrovert, sensing, intuitive, thinking, feeling, judging, and perceiving. Finally, in the late 1970s, Don Lowry created a metaphorical assessment based on the historical research dating back to Hippocrates, called True Colors. Don Lowry's True Colors translates complicated personality and learning theories into practical information in a fun and easy way to understand and use. The outcomes are represented as colors: *thinker-green, feeler-blue, doer-orange*, and *planner-gold.*

It is beneficial for the user to understand him/herself and others and learn how to relate based on those known characteristics and attributes. There are several personality assessments available to add to your self-awareness in your endeavor to learn about yourself (student of you). I recommend the True Colors assessment as a resource for your toolbox. It has the respected significance of research and the ease of common, everyday vernacular. It is an easy, entertaining, and user-friendly way to identify your full-color spectrum to better understand yourself and others. It represents an individual's pathway to self-esteem and confidence. It can be completed online at **www.truecolorsintl.com.**

Take it or any preferred personality assessment and record your results and relevant information that will help you understand yourself first, then others that you are in relationship with.

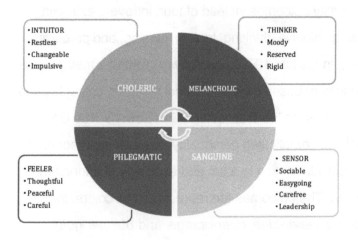

Personality Assessment Results and Revelations

_____

_____

_____

_____

_____

_____

_____

If you took the True Colors assessment, the high-est-scoring result (color) represents your strengths. Self-esteem will be derived from your first characteristic (color). Your second-highest scoring result (color) influences how you express your first. Although the third is a less significant indicator of your character, It still weighs in the balance of your color spectrum. Lastly, the fourth (color) represents your weaknesses and should be considered relevant to your understanding and perspective about who you are, how you represent yourself, and how you conduct yourself in relationships and situations. Knowing your own character traits will help you to understand yourself and how you relate to others better. Knowing your strengths will help you gain confidence in certain areas and boost your esteem. Knowing your weaknesses will help you to know where you might gain strength in others, especially if you work as part of a team or as a way of gaining balance and unity in your relationships.

Remember my story that was shared at the beginning of this journey? The references for my thoughts during my "mirror" experience are the result of messages that I have received over the years of my life. At some time in my life, I was told by some source or person (maybe even my own internal voice) that how I looked did not meet the societal standard of "*beauty*;" therefore, I was ugly and unacceptable, or less than others. Most of us have those references and use them as the basis for how we see ourselves. There are some exceptions; people whose nurturance included constant affirming and validating messages. These are the people who either have a healthy perspective of themselves or are on the extreme; narcissistic. Let's focus on the majority rather than the exceptions. Suppose these references that caused you to question or even doubt yourself are wrong, and your use of them is causing you undue stress or creating an incorrect perspective for how you see yourself? The spiritual arrest that blinded my eyes and muted my thoughts during the experience I shared was my "*awakening*." During that space in time, the Spirit of God corrected my messaging and reminded me of who I truly am. He assured me that I am *not* the container that I am wrapped in, but rather His light residing on the inside of me. He instructed me to get rid of the misinformation that I had subscribed to from the unreliable sources that I believed and to begin to see myself through His eyes. He allowed me to have a glimpse. It was *all light* and like nothing I have ever thought or imagined. For this reason, I compel you to do the same. Examine your perspective about yourself and all of the sources that have provided you references for how you see yourself. Do this exercise as a way of evaluating the credibility of those messages. Be prepared to focus on the "container" that carries *you*.

Container of You

Items needed:

Styrofoam Cup

Roll of Masking Tape

Writing Pen

When thinking about yourself and your self-worth, it is not uncommon to think less of yourself than others. It is more common to compare yourself to someone else or to someone else's standard.

Think for a moment of the styrofoam cup as your "worth," and remember the many messages you have heard about yourself over the years of your life. Are there any negative messages that have stuck with you over the years? For instance, have you ever been called "ugly," "fat," "bossy," "mean," and "angry"? Have you been told you are not smart enough, too aggressive, or intimidating? Have you believed your dad does not love you, or you are not wanted by your mom?

First, use the writing pen to write the words or short phrases you remember all over the outside of the cup. Write both positive and negative messages.

Now, direct your attention to the negative messages. Consider those messages as "leaks" in your self-esteem, and therefore your self-worth. Use your writing pen to punch a hole in the cup in every place where the negative words/phrases are written. Pay attention to the cup and the damage that allows your self-worth to drain out of you.

Now for a moment, consider the styrofoam cup as an analogy. It is a container that was designed and created with a specific purpose in the mind of its creator. Likewise, you were created with a specific purpose by your creator (Jeremiah 29:11). When the cup is damaged, it is unable to fulfill the purpose for which it was designed. Everything that is poured into it leaks out of the places where there is a deficit (hole). Likewise, the negative messages you have carried throughout your life are damage that inhibits your perspective about your worth and interferes with your ability to hold onto the good that is poured into your life, even interferes with you fulfilling your purpose. Regardless of your efforts to go to church, read positive material, receive positive information from other sources, if you do not attend to the damage done by the negative messages, you will struggle to achieve your intended purpose because of the constant drain.

There's hope; you can rescript the messages!

Start by using strips of the masking tape and cover each of the holes in the cup. Once finished, begin to reframe the messages into something positive that affirms and validates who you, based on how *the creator* sees you. This may require you to come to terms with the need to make some necessary changes. This exercise is about you changing your perspective so that you can ultimately change your outcome. The way you see yourself will influence how you present yourself in what you do and how you relate to others. It is life-impacting. This exercise is not about your physical wellness (physical wellness will be addressed during the Physical Quest). It is the first step in getting clear about your "*self*" definition so that you can be who you were designed to be.

Now, write your reframed messages on top of the masking tape where the covered holes and negative messages were once obvious. Do not stop until every message has been rewritten and a new message that affirms and validates what your worth is in its place. If you get stuck, use a Bible concordance or other credible reference to assist you in finding out what the source of "*truth*" says about you and your worth. You may need to do this work on a sheet of paper or in a journal to fully work through your new thoughts, affirmations, and truths. It is important to note that negative messages may be factual, i.e., "you are overweight" or "you are an angry person." Please be honest with yourself and own those truths.

In your effort to re-script those messages, identify what you need to do to make the desired changes so that you can be the authentic reference you desire. It may require seeking professional help and doing some deeper psychological and or emotional work. There may be costs, financially, physically, and even spiritually, but you are worth it!

Here are a few biblical examples of re-scripting:

You Say...	God Says...	Therefore...	Bible Reference
Nobody really loves me	I Love You	I am Loved by God	John 3:16 & John 3:34
I can't do it	You can do all things	I can do it	Philippians 4:13
It's not worth it	It will be worth it	All things work together for good	Romans 8:28
I am unforgiveable	I forgive you	I am forgiven	1 John 1:9 & Romans 8:1
I'm not smart enough	I give you wisdom	I am wise in Christ	1 Corinthians 1:30
I feel all alone	I will never leave you or forsake you	God is Always with me	Hebrews 13:5
I am afraid	I have not given you a spirit of fear	I will NOT Fear	2 Timothy 1:7

Acquiring new information about your self-worth will assist you in making different conclusions. Hopefully, you will cease measuring your worth against man-made standards and only use references from a credible source—the Creator.

It is important to note that sometimes the people who should be the most credible have to be discredited because of their own woundedness. Even a parent, spouse, sibling, or friend may have to lose their credibility status because they cannot give you what they do not have to give. Release them from that responsibility, forgive them, and love them from where they are. It may not be their fault that they were not able to fulfill that role in your life.

The Sexual Quest is the next mile in the journey of life. It is two-fold and requires that you first work out your relationship with yourself to gain clarity about who you are, who you want to be, and acceptance of the truth. Before you can prepare for a relationship with anyone else, you must first have a healthy relationship with yourself! Truth is the essential ingredient of every healthy relationship.

What do you know already about yourself?

_____

_____

_____

_____

_____

_____

_____

What characteristics, personality traits, and beliefs make you uniquely you?

_____

_____

_____

_____

_____

_____

_____

This process requires you to dig deep to discover likes and dislikes, your dreams and fears, your strengths and weaknesses. You will have to become a *"student* of *you"* first. Learning from the references that define and characterize you so that you can become the *"teacher* of *you;"* a self-assured educator of who you are and what you bring to your relationships—confident and resolved—ready for the connection with others when required.

You are constantly exposed to messages in the media, from your family and friends, from enemies, and even strangers. The messages are characteristic of their expectations or observations of you.

Where do you get your messages about who you are, i.e., media, words of others, negative self-talk, etc.?

_____

_____

_____

_____

_____

What do the messages say about you?

_____

_____

_____

_____

_____

Are they focused on the exterior references of you or the internal?

_____

_____

_____

_____

_____

Do the messages depict who you really are or only how others see you?

_____

_____

_____

Have you accepted the messages or rejected them?

_____

_____

_____

Are the messages based on truth?

_____

_____

_____

_____

This milestone requires you to come to some determinations about yourself. You were born of a man and woman, and your birth was the decision of others. Since you had nothing to do with your conception or birth, your initial life circumstances and experiences were outside of the realm of your control. You may have been born into a family of two parents who loved you and took seriously their responsibility to contribute to your development. You may have been born into this reality with only one actively involved parent. Maybe you were born to a mother who thought enough of you to ensure that you were placed in the care of someone else who was a more positive influence for you and consequently made a decision to give that someone responsibility and permission to parent you.

You may have been born to parents who were unprepared for the grand responsibility of parenting and therefore did not have the ability to give you what you needed because they did not have it themselves. Perhaps the very person(s) who were supposed to care for and protect you from harm, hurt you or allowed others to. They may have neglected, abandoned, or made decisions to cause you physical, emotional, mental, or even sexual abuse. Their decisions may have resulted in you being placed into a "system" that failed to provide a better alternative, causing you to have negative references for who you are and your value/ worth. There has to be a point in time when you make a conscious, deliberate decision to choose the reference that defines you for yourself. In the Sexual Quest, you have to consider the essence of who you are: your gender, identity, body image, self-esteem, self-concept, and confidence.

In 1995, before my LifeQuest™ journey begun, I

made a decision to cut all of the chemical relaxers from my hair. The decision was the result of a greater sense of self-awareness and desire to wear my hair in its natural state. It was a sort of rite of passage into myself by embracing the true essence of me, unbound by societal views of beauty. As I think about that transformation, I can hear the lyrics to "I Am Not My Hair" by India Aire playing in my mind. "I am not my hair; I am not this skin; I am not your expectations, no."

When I shared my story of survival from breast cancer, I talked about my "mirror" experience where I was faced with the full view of my image. I was undeniably a woman, but when faced with the effects of cancer and chemotherapy on my body, I had to resolve that I am still a woman regardless of the state of my anatomy. If I was only a woman because of my breast, my hair, or the image of my body before cancer, then who was I in that moment of truth when I became aware that I had no breast, my hair was gone, and the body image I had become accustomed to was undeniably changed? That was my point of decision. I decided right then and there to see myself through the eyes of God and to look beyond my flesh and all my flaws to see the real me.

Self-talk is also a powerful source of messaging that should be filtered. My frame of reference had to change, and I had to accept the truth of myself from a reliable source—my heavenly Father. All of my other references would have left me incomplete and lacking self-actualization. So many sources had convinced me that straight, long, non-kinky hair was beautiful. There were no references for bald on a woman being beautiful. There were sources in my awareness of full voluptuous breasts being more desirable and preferred. However, there I stood with a reflection of me that was unfamiliar and surprisingly the complete opposite of all of my associations of beauty. I desperately needed a new perspective.

When you look in the mirror, whom do you see? Do you see a healthy-sized and weighted person for the statue and frame that carries you? Like me, have your personal indications of beauty come from someone or something with a skewed view? The Sexual Quest has to consider that your body image may be distorted by an unhealthy perspective of eating. Your choice to eat too little or too much is reflective of how you see yourself and may need adjusting. This also includes other forms of self-mutilating behaviors that influence your option about your image. Unhealthy behaviors that change your physical image in any way should be processed during the Sexual Quest as part of identifying and accepting the authentic person of you.

When you look in the mirror, whom do you see? Do you

identify with the gender of the body you were born into? If there is a conflict with what you see and how you identify yourself, this is a point of decision for you. How you relate to yourself and others depends on your decision. Sexual identity has to be considered during the Sexual Quest because it is relevant to the person that you are. It will also be considered in other areas of LifeQuest™ as appropriate.

Have you been sexualized inappropriately as a result of a sexual assault or rape? Depending on your age and stage of development at the time of the offense, you may have acquired an unhealthy or inappropriate reference for sexual relations. If the offense was perpetrated by someone of the same sex or a person in a position of authority over you, this might have also caused confusion about your sexual identity. These are factors that should be taken into consideration as you determine who you are and transverse through the milestones of the Sexual Quest.

The debate about sexuality and gender differences is one that has continued for generations, and there is evidence that could be cited on both sides of the argument. It is not my intention to dictate how you should reconcile your sexuality and gender identity. However, if you choose to accept the Holy Bible as your source of truth, it is clear on the subject (Genesis 2:18-25, NIV). It was clear that a suitable helper was not an animal because the animals had already been created. It was not another man because the process used to create man (Adam) was not the same process used to make the suitable helper (named *wo*man because she was created from his womb). Like it or not, the Bible established the reference for man's helper (mate) as someone of the opposite gender. Any other union is considered unnatural and contrary to Scripture (source of truth). This truth has been known since the beginning of time but is rejected by some to satisfy the desires of the flesh (Romans 1:20-32). There are many people that I love and respect who are struggling with this matter. I want them to know that I love and respect them regardless, and so does God! Your identity is between you and Him.

Physical attributes are also part of your Sexual Quest because you should be comfortable in your own skin, and if you are not, you are more likely to compromise the content of the container. I am reminded of a time in my life when I was not very confident or comfortable in my skin. For most of my life, I was tall and thin, or what was referred to as "lanky." The unintended verbal references from my family, "skinny mini," "string bean," and other statements about my size and weight stuck with me. They were not complimentary, and the impact followed me into adulthood. When I married my husband, Michael, I lacked a strong self-concept. Even though I received compliments from admiring males and my husband was very vocal about his approval of my looks, my mindset had become fixed on the negative references that were my constant confirmation. The battle was in my mind; I struggled with my own thoughts about my beauty. Unfortunately, our society contributes to this issue for many of us.

The messages in the media about beauty are often skewed; white and light are more beautiful than dark, thin more than thick, and straight hair more desirable than curly or kinky. I am painfully aware of a woman who has spent her life trying to fit society's definition of beautiful. She has extremely unhealthy eating habits to try to keep her weight off. She has bleached her skin and damages her hair with all the chemicals she uses trying to keep the gray at bay, removing even the slightest hint of a wave or pigmentation from her natural texture and color. Worst still, she has gone to extreme measures with surgeries in an effort to correct anything that does not fit the beauty standard, including natural wrinkles and lines from the expression of life. Even as I write this, my emotions rise as I remember where I have come on this matter; settled with my natural, locked hair without even the use of chemicals to color the gray that started at fifteen years of age. I am far from "skinny mini" and embrace my curves, and the blessing of my height allows me the privilege of being able to stand tall in my confident self. Conversely, the other woman is now into her sixties and still expends overwhelming effort to keep her skin and hair washed out of color, her skin as tight as she can get it with creams and chemicals, and yet she still has no true affirmation of who she is and that she is beautiful—a sad fact.

Self-esteem is about esteeming yourself. Likewise, self-concept, self-image, self-identity all begin with "*self*." You determine the concept and image you identify with, and if it differs from the appearance of the body you reside in, you are at a point of decision.

There are essentially three things that you have control over, what you think, what you say, and what you do, which includes; actions you initiate and your responsive actions (how you respond to what is done or said by others). While you do not have control over others or events that may affect you, you do have responsive control. For this reason, the Sexual Quest requires you to investigate your beliefs about who you are and to take responsibility and ownership for your choice to believe what messages you will subscribe to. Additionally, choose how you will respond to the uncontrollable circumstances of your life.

The choices are to surrender to the tragic events of your life or persevere by pressing through and overcoming them. "We overcome by the blood of the Lamb *and* the word of our testimony" (Revelation 12:11, NKJV). God has done His part by choosing to go to the cross and shedding His blood for us. He declared in scripture, "I came that they may have life and have it abundantly" (John 10:10, ESV). Our part, should we choose to accept it; (1) believe that God is the Creator and giver of the "gift" of life, (2) believe that He died to purchase the gift of life for us, and (3) share our story (testimony) of how we have overcome our life circumstances with others who may be struggling with the same or similar realities. Every time we share our story with another, we get stronger, and we also offer hope to others who are in the struggle to overcome.

Redefining ourselves solidifies our new identity in Christ. Delete the old images and descriptors and rewrite those using new messages that are better aligned with the "real" you. "Therefore if anyone is in Christ, he is a new creation: old things have passed away; behold, all things have become new" (2 Corinthians 5:17, NKJV).

Perception is defined as "the basic component in the formation of a concept." Without a doubt, your perception influences your thoughts and beliefs about life. The things you have been deliberately taught and what you have learned coincidentally are your perceptions. They are the basis for your reality and ultimately become your perspective, "theory of your understanding of the reference-your belief."

I think about it this way, what I receive through my experiential references, teachings, and cultural conditioning, I perceive, and they are my perceptions. My perceptions establish the foundation for my belief, which is my perspective. Here is a visual display.

What you *receive* → you *perceive* → you *believe* = your *perception* which ultimately becomes what you put into practice → your *perspective.*

You have a point of decision; what will you do to right the wrong references of your past in order to form the best reference for your future? Whatever the circumstances of your conception and birth, the decision was made for you to live, and so you are here. Even if your beginning in life was *hell*, you are still here and what happens next is *your* decision. With no disregard for your unfortunate beginning, regardless of where or how you started, this is a point of decision. If you have allowed your present and future to be dictated by the past, *stop*! Decide now to gain a truthful perspective about who you are and the purpose for your life, then choose to connect your journey with the life you desire—*LifeQuest™*.

If your beginning has set you up for success, are you on the course of life that is sure to lead you to your destiny? If not, make a decision now to make the turns that will put you on the right path and get in the quest for life. It is a journey that is divinely charted by God to carry you to your purpose.

When you respect yourself and others-being awake

to who you are and who you are not, you are healthy. The opposite of healthy is denial. Make it your personal goal to be aware every day of your life. When you are aware, you are able to interact with life as it happens and take an active role in the outcome.

In spite of what you have experienced, you are valuable, and God can and will use you for His divine purpose. I am reminded of Malachi 3:3 (ESV), "He will sit as a refiner and purifier of silver, and he will purify the sons of Levi and refine them like gold and silver…" I heard a story about a woman in the late 1800s who visited a silversmith to observe the process of making silver. She noted that the silversmith had to sit in front of a hot fire and hold the silver over the hottest part of the fire allowing it to heat up. It sounds like God is allowing you to be refined in the fire of life. The story continues with the lady questioning the silversmith about his decision to endure the heat and if it is possible to accomplish the task in another way. The silversmith told her that he not only had to sit in the heat of the fire, but he had to constantly watch over the metal while it is in the fire to ensure that the flames do not destroy it. If it is left in the fire a moment too long, it would be destroyed. She asked, "How do you know when the silver is fully refined?" He responded with absolute certainty, "The refining process is complete when I can see my image in it!" Again, this is a parallel of God allowing you to be refined in the process of life. He is sitting in the heat of the fire, holding you and watching closely to ensure that you are simply re-fined but not destroyed! He is watching for His image to be revealed in you.

If you accept that God is the creator, He made you "fear-fully and wonderfully" (Psalm 139:14, NIV). Take the good, discard the bad and the things that you are uncertain about, give them to the Lord. Choose to love yourself! It is difficult to truly love a stranger, even when that stranger is yourself. Once you are confirmed in yourself, your soul mate will be ready for you, not before. The order matters!

Reflection

Think about the exercise you completed in the *discovery* section with the Styrofoam cup (container of *you*). It is one common-sense way to process your references for who you are and to choose your own definition. The very thought-provoking exercise using the styrofoam cup is an analogy of the usefulness and purpose of a container. Theoretically, a styrofoam cup was created with a specific purpose; to be a container. More precisely, if you consider its design that includes an insulating material, it was created to hold hot liquid. However, if the structure of the cup were compromised by holes, it would no longer be capable of fulfilling the purpose for which it was created. In fact, if you poured the hot liquid into this container in its diminished capacity, you may even cause injury to the person closest to it by the spillage of hot liquid through the damaged places.

Likewise, if you consider yourself a container (container of *you*) that was created with a purpose, designed to hold good things, and the damage caused to your container, the messages you have heard or experienced over the years of your life, you too could cause emotional injury to someone you are the closest in a relationship because you; yourself are hurting. You've heard the expressions "hurting people, hurt people," or "misery loves company"? These are both references for what happens when a hurting person tries to have a relationship with someone.

Take some time to reflect on the messages on your cup and their source; media (printed, visual, and audible), family, friends, society in general, and even your own internal thinking-self-talk. As you recall the messages you have captured on the outside of the cup, and the reframed messages written on the masking tape, consider the styrofoam cup as a representative of the "container of *you*." Like the cup in its actual state, it demonstrates the same inability to hold the good things that are poured in and is also unable to fulfill the divine purpose for which you were created due to the drain of your needed contents through the deficits in your container, caused by acceptance of the negative messages (emotional damage). As you focus on self-help, reading books, listening to positive messages, attending church, seminars, and other sources of inspiration, you will not have the capacity to retain and apply the good that is poured into you unless you attend to the damage, hurt, and brokenness that exists.

What negative messages were revealed through your "container of *you*" activity? Write the initial message, source of the message, whether it is a deficit or value to you, and then re-scripted a new message that is valuable and more appropriate to you and that you will accept.

Message	Source	Value (+/-)	New Message

Is there a conflict with whom you think you are and what
you see reflected in the mirror when you look at yourself? If
so, what is the conflict, and where did it originate?

_____

_____

_____

_____

What are some of the images reflected to you in the mirror that you are capable of changing to more accurately reflect who you are? How will you change them?

_____

_____

_____

_____

_____

_____

Consider the source of your messages. Are those sources trustworthy/valued/respected? If so, process them as truth and make the necessary changes. If not, determine them to be lies from the enemy, meant to kill, steal, and destroy you (John 10:10) and discard them as the destructive intentions they are sent to be.

Ephesians 2:10 says, "We are God's workmanship, created in Christ Jesus to do good works, which God prepared in advance for us to do." If you accept this as truth, you must discard anything that conflicts with this truth.

What has to change in your perception in order for your perspective to be changed, allowing you to see yourself through God's eyes as someone with worth and value?

_____

_____

_____

_____

_____

_____

You control what you say, think, do, and how you respond to the uncontrollable.

Resolve

I believe that God loves me personally. He knows me because He made me. He has established my value and worth. My life came at a high price, and He paid for it with His blood! He did not make a mistake when He allowed me to be in this life, and He is aware of the circumstances of my existence. He knew my story before it began, and He gave me everything I needed to endure. I believe Romans 8:28 (ESV), "And we know that for those who love God *all* things work together for good, for those who are *called* according to *his purpose*." Thank you, Lord, for choosing me and making me wonderfully.

SEXUAL QUEST PART TWO

Relationship with Significant Other

Affirmation

"A Marriage may be made in heaven, but the maintenance must be done on earth."

Scriptures

"Love is patient, kind…bears all things, believes all things, hopes all things, endures all things. Love never fails."

1 Corinthians 13:4-8 (NIV)

"Submitting yourselves one to another in the fear of God."

Ephesians 5:21 (KJV)

"Nevertheless let everyone of you in particular so love his wife even as himself; and the wife see that she reverences her husband."

Ephesians 5:33 (NIV)

Prayer

Lord, as I advance in this Sexual Quest to consider my relationship with the person you have for me to relate to intimately, help me to search myself, and put my focus on making the changes needed in me for the health of my intimate relationship. I believe that the success of an intimate relationship (marriage) is not in finding the right person but in being the right person. I can be the right person with your guidance. Grant me your peace in the process of waiting for the person *you* have so ordained for me and for your timing. I am committed to working on myself and allowing you to work on the other person. When you determine that we are both ready, connect our lives and allow us, as two whole individuals, to relate in a healthy way, and then me. Make us one in you. Amen.

Objectives

- Review the *discovery* exercises from the previous session and note the outcomes.
- Use what you have discovered about yourself in the first part of the Sexual Quest and apply it to consideration for an intimate relational connection to another person.
- In your self-awareness, become less judgmental and critical of your partner, choosing to be the "*student*," learning about the other person while being the "*teacher* of *you*" to that person.
- Become more prepared to facilitate positive communication with the other person, effectively dealing with conflict as an opportunity for discovery.

Discovery

Five Love Languages by Gary Chapman

Author Gary Chapman has designed an assessment called *5 Love Languages* that is an ideal reference for getting to know how you communicate love and how your intimate partner communicates love. The assessment is available online at **www.5lovelanguages.com.** Please complete the assessment and record your Love Languages based on your highest to lowest scores.

1st Love Language

_____

_____

2nd Love Language

_____

_____

3rd Love Language

_____

_____

4th Love Language

_____

_____

5th Love Language

_____

_____

   Your highest scoring Love Language is the one that you hear the loudest. It resonates with you as love and is clearly understood when expressed. Your next highest is complimentary of the second and may also get an admired response. As the scores lessen, the significance is less effective. This does not mean that you will not appreciate your loved one doing the dishes for you if your number one language is Quality Time instead of Acts of Service. It just means that scheduling time to snuggle on the couch to watch a movie together would say "I love you" more loudly and more clearly.

   Now that you have settled your relationship with yourself, part two will take what you have learned to the place of decision about your most intimate internal relationship with a spouse, committed partner, or promised potential. The second part of the Sexual Quest is about sharing what you know about yourself (*teacher* of *you*) and learning the intimate details of that person (*student* of the other person). You will examine your relational history for healthy references for intimate connections to draw some perspectives and determinations about how those exchanges have influenced your behavior in other intimate relationships. In doing so, you will be able to identify the compatibilities and incompatibilities, communicate your relational preferences, and make necessary collaborations, not compromises, for how to navigate current and future relationships more confidently. What are the "deal makers" and "deal breakers"? What are the issues that should be discussed and worked out before marriage or in order to advance to the next level in the relationship in a healthy way?

Before I married my husband, Michael, I had eight marriage proposals (don't judge me, keep reading). The first at age fifteen by me; I believed I was in love with the person of Michael Devon Mays. He was the middle of five sons in a military family that my family met while stationed at Castle Air Force Base in California. My family lived across the street from the Mays, and our parents' friendship turned out to be a lifetime relationship. Even after our departure from Castle, my parents remained connected to the Mays. We settled in Texas and the Mays in Louisiana. On occasional trips to Alabama to visit family on my father's side, we would stop to visit with the Mays family.

During the summer of 1981, my mother, sister, and I visited the Mays family. By that time, both families had experienced divorce, so the visit was between our mothers. All of the boys were still living at the house but were all older and had their own lives and social schedules. Entertaining two adolescent girls was the least of their concerns. However, Michael, being the person he was and still is, made it his responsibility to show us a good time. He had a construction job and worked hard in the scorching LA sun, but came home after his day of work, showered, and was a gracious host to my sister and me. He took us to movies, skating, introduced us to his friends around the neighborhood, and anything else we desired to do on our vacation. I fell in love with his spirit of generosity and, subsequently, the character he presented to us.

At the end of our 1981 summer vacation, I was certain that I was in love, and I proposed to the man that unknowingly would eventually be my husband. Of course, he declined. He was and still is a very practical person and gave all of the logical reasons why we could not get married; our age, his inability to provide for himself or me, and his pending departure for college that would put even more distance between us. I wanted to be his wife, and he wanted to be my brother/friend. Needless to say, we did not get married at that time. Unknowingly, my parent's divorce and the absence of my father during my most influential years were doing an emotional number on me. As I matriculated high school and the challenges of relationships and dating, I experienced several more proposals.

Proposal two was from an older guy that was much more mature than me. Our courtship was brief, innocent, and sweet. He respected me and my decision for celibacy. Since my position at that time was that sex was for marriage, he proposed. It was too much, too soon, and I declined. The third, fourth, and fifth proposals were all from the same person. I was still in high school, young, foolish, and unable to see beyond his obvious issues and our collective immaturity. Thank God for my father, who would not give his blessing for this union, and for my respect for my father that kept me from proceeding without it.

Off to college, I went with proposal six looming. This time I believed that I was ready. He was also an older guy that I should have never been involved with, but because I lacked true self-confidence and did not value myself enough, I bought into his game and became a subject of his affection. I believed that he would make me his bride, and I allowed myself to become intimate with him, mistaking the physical intimacy as love. The experience resulted in the conception of my beautiful and cherished daughter, Carmon, the promise of marriage, and a ring, but no marriage. This relationship cost me much more than I ever expected to pay. I compromised my own values and my body to someone who did not deserve me or the love and commitment that I intended for marriage. This is a lesson that came with emotional baggage that had to be dealt with during my own personal Emotional Quest. My story is an all too familiar saga that far too many women have lived. Knowing and loving God does not ensure you won't make poor decisions. However, it does guarantee that all things, even the outcomes of our sins, He can use for good (Romans 8:28).

With Carmon as a reality check for my life and purpose, I was no longer willing to take chances with her life, so that meant that I had to be more deliberate with my own. As I stood on the spiritual foundation that was established by my parents during my formative years, I declared that I would wait on The Lord and commit to unite my life and Carmon's with the man that God had planned for us. With no idea who that would be, I focused on my education and did not attend to social relationships that would distract me from the goal of self-improvement. I had another life that depended on me being self-assured and confident. I was her reference for being a woman, being successful, and accomplished. I did not want her sights to be set lower than they should. The pressure was real!

Interestingly enough, when I was not looking for a husband, he was looking for me. The Bible says, "He who finds a wife, finds a good thing, and obtains favor from the Lord" (Proverbs 18:22, NKJV). I had come to realize that I was a "good thing," and I prayed for God's intervention because with my record, I no longer trusted my own judgment. However, I was not expecting the manifestation of his blessing to come so quickly or in the way that it did.

Remember proposal number two from the respectful, more mature guy? Well, he was back a second time, still committed to his intentions of making me his wife. The fact that I was a single mother made it very clear that I had not kept my commitment to celibacy, but he still maintained his love for me and reaffirmed his desire to marry me and accept the complete package of my reality. I thought, *He must be my husband—the one that I prayed for and that The Lord has sent as His answer!* So I accepted his proposal (number seven) and his assignment to Greece that came with it. He was in the United States Air Force and was home on leave (vacation) between his assignments. The next one would take him to Athens, Greece. With my father's blessing, I accepted his proposal, and Carmon and I joined him there.

Two weeks before our departure, my best friend—pseudo brother, and one true love, Michael (proposal number one), returned to the states from an assignment overseas in Italy. We had kept in touch and shared the joys and pains of each other's lives over the years. I told him of my upcoming plans to move to Greece, where I would marry the man of my prayers. Being a military man himself, Michael cautioned against this plan. He explained that it was not an easy process for Americans to get married in foreign countries and suggested I get married in the US; more specifically, my hometown, with all of my family and friends witnessing in celebration. While Michael's suggestion made perfect sense and would have been my preference, time was not on my side. Because my proposed future husband was only home for a brief time, my options were to marry sooner by doing it in a foreign county or waiting for the ceremonial nostalgia on a future date when he could earn enough leave time to return to the states for a wedding. Enter *compromise*... I chose option one and set the plans in motion to get our passports, shipped our belongings, and moved to Greece.

In the meantime, Michael and I enjoyed our reunion. We laughed and reminisced about our past experiences and future dreams. Our conversations were easy, and we related well. It was so naturally right, and the chemistry was undeniable. To my surprise, I was again like the fifteen-year-old girl, in love, and resolved that this was my

126

husband. Only this time, Michael was also convinced and so convinced that he purchased a ring and became my eighth proposal.

I questioned God—which one is the answer to my prayer? Within just two weeks of each other, two men from my past had returned to my life at a time when I was not looking for them, but they were apparently in search of me. Everything was set for me to go to Greece; tickets were purchased, passports in hand, apartment leased, and my proposal was waiting for Carmon and me to arrive. I even had both of my parent's blessings. I was truly conflicted. I needed some confirmation that I was making the "right" decision. It could not just be about my emotion or even the outward appearances. I loved them both, and they had each demonstrated their love and respect for not only me but for my daughter.

I was looking for confirmation and decided to ask my mother for her perspective. Her advice convicted me; how could I accept a man's proposal and then change my mind so easily. My decision was made; Carmon and I were going to Greece. Waiting for *divine* confirmation is highly recommended! He may not come when you want Him, but He is *always* on time. God's grace is so sufficient.

I arrived in Greece on August 8, 1987. It was summer and the time of European vacation, which meant all of the government offices in the country were closed for the season. The legal consummation of our relationship would have to wait until September, when the government offices resumed business.

While we waited, I became painfully aware of the effects that life in the military and the prolonged exposure to trauma had on my proposed. He was changed, and despite his affection for me and his admirable intentions, I was now certain that he was not the "right" one. He had diagnosable issues that were provoked by the innocent cries of my young daughter. My revelation came in the midst of a violent episode with him. I was far from home but not far from the Lord when it occurred to me that I had acted in haste and had not waited for the true confirmation that would have come from my heavenly Father if I had been patient enough to wait for it. By God's grace, Carmon and I returned safely to the United States and to the man who was the true manifestation of God's answer to my prayer, Michael Devon Mays. Although we were confirmed in our intentions, we allow time for our courtship and relationship to progress, and we honored my earthly father's request to allow some time before pursuing marriage. While we waited, I completed my undergraduate degree and advanced my self-confidence. We were married on June 4, 1988, without regret.

This is a great time to distinguish between compromise vs. collaboration. As a professional who works with relationships for a living and mediator, I am aware of the frequent use of the word compromise as it relates to getting along with others or dealing with conflict. It is my understanding that this word is often used with intentions of signifying the willingness to give in or let go of something for the sake of agreement or resolve. While the intentions are commendable, the truth is the practice of compromise is a win/lose rather than a win/win outcome. You would never hear the word compromise when negotiating an agreement in a business deal. The business industry's word choice, collaboration, indicates an agreement to work to have a win/win outcome: one where both sides walk away from the transaction with something of significance. This understanding has revolutionized my thinking about more intimate relationships, and I constantly teach my clients to approach their decisions and interactions with others, especially their spouse or significant other, collaboratively. Just the perspective of a winning outcome changes the dynamic of the interaction.

In preparation for the second part of the Sexual Quest, I will share a letter that was written by an anonymous person. It is a love letter that appears to be from God. It reads:

Dear Child,

Everyone longs to give herself completely to someone, to have a deep soul relationship with another, to be loved thoroughly and exclusively. But I say to you: No, not until you are satisfied with giving yourself totally and unreservedly to Me will you be capable of the perfect relationship that I have planned for you. Not until you are satisfied with having an intensely personal and unique relationship with Me alone, discovering that in Me, your satisfaction is to be found. You will never be united with another until you are united with Me, exclusive of anyone or anything else, exclusive of any desire or longing. I want you to stop planning, stop wishing, stop listening to others, and allow Me to give you the most thrilling plan in existence, one that you cannot imagine. I want you to have the best! Please… allow me to bring it to you. You, just wait! That's all. Don't be anxious. Don't worry. Don't look around at others and the things they have or the things I have given them. Don't look at the things you think you want. You just keep watching Me, expecting the greatest things. Keep listening and learning the things I tell you. You just keep looking at Me, for if you don't, you will miss all the things I want to show you. *And…* when you are ready, I'll surprise you! With a love far more wonderful than you can ever imagine. You see, until the one I have for you is ready (I am working now, at this very moment, to have you both ready at the same time), and until you are satisfied exclusively with Me and the life I have prepared for you, you won't be able to experience the love that exemplifies your relationship with Me. The marital and concrete union of body, mind, and soul, the perfect agape love that I offer you. Be satisfied, My sweet child- with My perfect love. When you are running as fast as you can towards Me, the person I have to be your mate will be running as fast as you are towards me too.

Having God as your first love is a sure way to prepare for loving someone else and knowing if that person loves you the way you should be loved. It is a good idea to do some inventory of your former relationships and gain some insight about what was right or wrong about them. Why did they not work? It is futile to continue to find yourself in romantic relationships where there is intimacy but no true love.

The second part of the Sexual Quest involves the most intimate relationship you have or will have besides the one you have with God. This relationship is with the person who will occupy the top shelf of your life, and it is your decision to place him/her there. For some of you, this is the person you are married to currently. For others, this is the person you will marry eventually (when you are both ready for that level of commitment and responsibility). Still, others may never marry this person and never experience the most intimate connection possible between two individuals. If your choice is to marry, the person you choose is the only relative you will have that is your choice. Think about it, your parents, siblings, and even your children are a result of consequences you did not control. Unless you adopted your child(ren), you did not even have control over the child(ren) you ended up with; you got what you got, like it or not. I also recognize that in some cultures, marriage is an arrangement, not a choice. Acknowledging this exception, in most cases, the person you marry is your choice.

I am reminded of my pregnancy with my youngest daughter. Michael and I were so excited in anticipation of this child and in conversation, agreed that we simply desired a healthy baby. We had not really spent much time discussing our gender preferences but silently prayed for a boy since we already had a daughter. The day came when we went for a prenatal appointment that included the first ultrasound examination. When the doctor asked if we wanted to know the sex of the baby, I answered yes, and

Michael answered, "Only if it's a boy." The doctor paused in light of the conflicting responses, turned to me, and said, "Well, I guess I am only talking to you." As the reality of his words registered in Michael's consciousness, he exclaimed his disappointment by saying, "Aww, man!" I was devastated, and he quickly realized the error of his words. We both desired to have a son, but we were not in control of the outcome of the gender of our child. For the record, we are extremely grateful that God blessed us with Chryston Dorvon, a girl!

As you consider your most intimate internal relationship with your spouse, committed partner, or promised potential, your role is to be the "teacher of *you*," as learned through the initial phase of the Sexual Quest. When you accept the responsibility to teach others about you and learn from others about them, you must commit to share what you know about yourself, freely and honestly, so that confusion and pretense are dispelled. In doing so, the other person does not have to fill in the blanks with assumptions. Decidedly, learning the intimate details of who that person is and what he or she aspires to become makes you a relational student. Consequently, if you fail to learn from your mistakes, you could be resigned to repeat them. It is wise to apply what you have learned from your past relational errors to your new relationships.

Since we are in a constant state of becoming who we are, if we neglect to share the newness of ourselves with those closest to us, we will soon find ourselves separated by the unfamiliar—let me be more clear. If you have an experience today that changes your perspective or influences, a difference in your philosophy about life, and you implement that change or insight into your existence, causing you to make different decisions or adjust your choices and behaviors, you cease to be the person that you were yesterday. Then tomorrow or next week offers another opportunity that further refines or reshapes who you are, and this continues over time; it will not be long before the person that you were relentless to the person that you are becoming. If you desire for your chosen "*top shelf*" person to know and grow with you, you will have to share with him/her who you are becoming and bring him/her along in your journey if s/he is willing to go.

Conversely, if you are changing, and developing new ideas, and subscribing to new philosophies as you grow in life and neglect to update your intimate partner's awareness of who you are becoming or if this most intimate person chooses not to grow with you; eventually you will reach a point of decision. Either you will abandon your growth to be in the place of stagnation with that person, him delaying your advancement to wait for him/her, or you will continue growing in the hope that s/he will catch up; knowing that if s/he chooses to go a different direction or to remain in the distance, the two of you may not overcome the separation and a decision about your future would be eminent. Remember that you cannot control others, only yourself. It is your choice; choose wisely.

Determine the compatibilities and incompatibilities in your relationship and address them directly through effective communication with your intimate person. Identify the differences between the two of you and decide to collaborate about what accommodations are necessary. I do not recommend compromise because it literally means someone loses and someone wins. Collaboration is a win/win arrangement. Are there non-negotiables for you? If so, identify them, own them, and speak them in truth to your intimate person.

Discuss the issues that should be worked out before marriage or in order to advance to the next level in the relationship and for the relationship to be healthy. Is marriage the next best advancement in the relationship? Sometimes we are so quick to follow the expectations of others that we "compromise" our own desires, and we end up being the one who loses. Marriage is not for everyone, and accepting someone else's blueprint could detour or, worst, derail the progress in your life journey.

How do you communicate your love, and how do you say "I love you" to another? If you are unaware of your language of love, it is possible that you are speaking in a foreign, unfamiliar way to the person you love. There are many references for how women and men relate to each other. Many books have been written based on research about the uniqueness of men vs. women. With the expressed written permission of Gary Chapman, I referenced the contributions of his work in "The Five Love Languages" for the benefit of illustrating this quest. His work relates a simplistic way to express your heartfelt commitment to your mate by using a personal assessment tool. You should have already completed the "free" assessment in the "Discovery" section. If not, please complete it online at www.5lovelanguages.com and document your results. The results will indicate your primary language of love as

1. Words of Affirmation
2. Quality Time
3. Receiving Gifts
4. Acts of Service
5. Physical Touch

The book is a highly recommended tool for your relational toolbox. If you know that the language you are speaking is not one your partner connects with, it is helpful to learn and use the one that does. Refer to Gary Chapman's website (https://www.5lovelanguages.com/) and book for explanations of each of the 5 Love Languages.

Now take some time to consider your relationship background and qualifications. Note the first romantic relationship in your memory—it is likely your parents. Were they married? If not, there is your first missing piece of information. If your parents were not married, where did you see your first picture of romantic love? Was it of your mother or father dating first one person and then another, and another, and another? Or did they cohabitate but never commit to marriage, again skewing your relational reference for romantic love. Maybe your parents were married, but they did not know how to relate well, so your visual reference for romantic relating was not very romantic. Instead, you saw two people who said they love each other. However, they hurt, dominated, or manipulated each other, a recurring demonstration of selfishness. Perhaps your family dynamic was of one sole parent and no picture of a healthy dual relationship. Whatever the case, your first reference for a romantic relationship is the catalyst for every future relationship. This is no to say that there are not exceptions for every reference; there are. This is simply to get you thinking about what your personal references are that have shaped your perspective and to encourage you to assess whether you need a different picture in order to help you draw your own more clearly.

I have story after story after story of marriages that have stood the test of time, twenty, thirty, sixty, even seventy-plus years. You are like me, probably thinking— *wow*—what a great testament to stay together for so many years. The truth is that those stories are of longevity, but not all of them are romantic. The marriages did not end in divorce but ended nonetheless. If you have a reference of your parents in a marriage by name only and there were no visual indications of love and care between them, your reference is still skewed. Consider your source and how it has influenced your relational dynamic. Do you like what you see, or do you need to fine-tune it?

Take a few moments to think about all of your relational references and what messages you have learned about intimacy and your role in a romantic relationship.

Parents

_____

_____

_____

_____

Other adults in your life (i.e., grandparents, aunts, friend's parents)

_____

_____

_____

_____

_____

Your first romantic relationship

_____

_____

_____

_____

_____

Dating relationships

_____

_____

_____

_____

_____

Movie or media romance

_____

_____

_____

_____

_____

Your marriage(s)

_____

_____

_____

_____

_____

Can you determine from your references if you have a healthy perspective about romance and intimacy in a relationship?

    I often tell my clients as a reminder, "In the journey of life, if you are working on yourself and the other person is also working, you will both make positive improvements together for the good of the relationship." However, "if you are working on yourself, but the other person is stagnated or going in a different direction than you, before long you will look around and become aware that the person you were traveling with is no longer beside you." You will find yourself at a point of decision—either you continue your self-improvements hoping the other person will catch up to you, become stagnate while you wait for the person to catch up, abandon your progress to go back to the place where you left that person, or realize that the person lacks motivation and drive or has no intentions of making self-improvements and as a result, your relationship will be out of sync. You have heard it before, "We just grew apart." Relationships are hard work, especially marriage, even under the most ideal circumstances. The commitment takes work. When adding the challenge of incompatibility or relational estrangement, it is a formula for irreconcilable differences; and likely inappropriate extramarital relationships or divorce.

The truth is that you are becoming a new person daily. Yesterday you had an experience or were exposed to a concept or theory that you agreed with. Because of that newly acquired way of thinking, you have changed beliefs, adjusted behaviors, and adopted a different personal conviction or philosophy for your life. That same process continues daily, and consequently, over time, you have become a different person. The process may be viewed as maturity, personal growth, or some form of self-improvement. The only challenge with that process is the failure to update the other person you are in a relationship with so that he or she is aware of the changes and can adjust accordingly. If you are the only one in the relationship who knows what you know, the other person is at a disadvantage. You have to be the "*teacher* of *you*" because you are the resident expert on "*you.*" You are living with yourself daily, experiencing life, and hopefully applying what you have learned. The only way someone else knows is by you sharing it with him or her.

It is not safe for you to share yourself with just anybody. You should be selective. If you are continually giving yourself away to anyone who will take a piece of you, it will not be long before you feel the deficit and the emptiness. Proverbs 4:35 (NLT) cautions to "guard your heart above all else because it determines the course of your life." These are clear instructions to proceed with caution when entering a relationship. Part two of the Sexual Quest will include sharing what you have learned about yourself with someone that you deem worthy of an intimate relationship with you. This requires you to accept your role in the relationship as the "*teacher* of *you,*" sharing information with this person about who you are over time and helping the other person to know and relate well with you. "Over time" is an important distinction! Courtship seems to be an age-old concept. There was a time in history when courtship was respected and adhered to the process for determining compatibility for marriage and was taking seriously. Now we have evolved to speed dating, virtual acquaintances, and even marriage at first sight. The courtship has been curtailed or eliminated, and the marriage expedited, the instant gratification route through the Sexual Quest. There is something to be said for slowing down and really getting to know each other before making the commitment of a lifetime. My intent is not to discount the diverse ways and means for getting acquainted with someone but rather to question the decision to circumvent the courtship process. There is necessary value in investing the time to get to know the person and having him or her get to know you, allowing time to ensure that each of you is in your respective roles and confirming compatibility.

A common assignment given to clients I am seeing for marital discord is to go on a date and get reacquainted. It seems trivial, but the reality is that couples take an active interest in each other while dating, but once they are married, they fall into the monotony of marriage and lose sight of the value in dating and keeping the relationship alive and thriving. The simple act of spending quality time together, undistracted by the TV, social media, housework, the kids, etc., can be enough to keep the thrill of the marriage going. It certainly offers the benefit of intentional updates for each of you to learn about the changes happening in the other.

Reflection

As you reflect on the relational references you have noted above for intimacy, are there any trends to note? If you were honest with yourself, what has been your role and the role of the other person in your past relationships? At the risk of offending someone, I will refer to the roles as "adult," "child," or "parent." I do not mean to literalize these titles; however, they are titles that are easily understood and illustrated. Keep an open mind and consider what role you have played and what the role of the other person has been.

The "adult" in the relationship takes responsibility for his or her actions and decisions, allowing the other person to have ownership appropriately for his or hers. Conversely, the "child" externalizes by deferring responsibility for his or her actions or decisions, makes excuses for shortcomings, is unwilling to respond in a mature way when faced with challenges, and like a child; blames others, whines about things not going his or her way, and thinks primarily of self. Finally, the "parent" internalizes by assuming all or most of the responsibility for what is wrong in the relationship, absolving the other person of his or her responsibility, consequently, is an enabler and perpetuates the problem.

Take some time to reflect on the past romantic relationships you have had in your life. List them below and indicate your role and the role of the other person in that relationship (adult, child, or parent). I have provided an example with the relationships indicated by the proposals that I shared previously.

Example

NAME	HIS ROLE (A/C/P)	MY ROLE (A/C/P)
Proposal 1	A	C
Proposal 2	A	C
Proposal 3, 4, 5	C	P
Proposal 6	C	P
*Proposal 7	A	A
Marriage	A	A

Although Proposal seven was characteristically an adult, he had undiagnosed Post Traumatic Stress (PTS). It interfered with his ability to be the "right" connection for me. With intervention and professional help, he could be a good mate for someone else.

Any combination other than an "adult" to "adult" relationship is unhealthy. No responsible person wants to be romantically intimate with an adult behaving like a child. As consenting adults, each person must bring their maturity and personal responsibility, and accountability to the relationship in order for it to be balanced and complete. Multiple references in scripture say it this way, "and the two became one flesh." From the beginning of creation, when God performed surgery on Adam, removed his rib to create woman, He declared that they were to be one—unified. No longer individuals, but unified and committed so deeply that they are one (Genesis 2:24, NIV). He continued to make the same point when questioned by the Pharisees about divorce. He contended that the only reason He permitted Moses to declare a written bill of divorce was due to the hardness of man's heart (selfishness/unforgiveness), but even then He reminded them that from the beginning, His intention is for man and woman to be one (unselfish and considerate of the other) (Mark 10:2-8). He goes on in Ephesians 5:21-31 (NIV) to explain the roles of husbands and wives, declaring that each is to submit themselves to the other out of reverence for God. He gives the reference of His own love for His bride (the Church) and the sacrifice of His body (life) for her. He actually died to His flesh in order to show His ultimate love for us (the Church-the Bride of Christ). This is not a formula for half and half. It is a compilation for two whole individuals to join together to create a union-oneness, without selfish regard, but with selfless disregard.

It is interesting that the scripture references two people as "flesh" and states that they become only one "flesh." I believe it is relevant to note that God does not deal with us in the flesh, but rather He deals with our spirit. The fact that the biblical union of marriage will not accommodate two people being in their own separate flesh, which I would refer to as "selfishness," is an indication that we have to be willing to become one flesh before we are ready to be married.

In every memory I have of marital discord, mine or clients, the issue usually comes down to someone being selfish and inconsiderate of the other person. This is true in the instance of infidelity, ineffective communication, and other presenting issues for marital counseling. When the couple is willing to refocus their attention, efforts, and emotions on pleasing the other person in the relationship, the union gets back in sync, and harmony is restored in the relationship.

Resolve

I am aware that I have been out of my role in my past relationships. I have been the _____, and I should have been the adult. I have allowed the other person to be the _____ instead of the adult. Today I vow to take responsibility for my role in my relationships. I will be the adult, taking ownership of my issues and dealing with them in a mature way. I will no longer accept my significant other blaming me or overshadowing me when decisions in our relationship require both our input and consent. Even when my opinions and contributions are not popular or agreed with, I will state them truthfully and will listen to the reasonable contributions of the other person and respond respectfully. I will communicate openly and be transparent to establish trust and affirm the relationship. I will not move too quickly through the courtship and will wait on godly confirmation before making a lifetime commitment.

SOCIAL QUEST

Horizonal-External
Relationships

Affirmation

"During times of crisis, we turn to people with whom we share our deepest connections to re-group and remind ourselves that we are part of a family or community and that our purpose in life remains intact."

Kenneth R. Ginsburg, MD

Scriptures

"In the same way, let your light shine before others, so that they may see your good works and give glory to your Father who is in heaven."

Matthew 5:16 (ESV)

"As iron sharpens iron, so one man sharpens another."

Proverbs 27:17 (ESV)

And you shall love the Lord your God with all your heart and with all your soul, and with all your mind, and with all your strength. The second is this: "You shall love your neighbor as yourself." There is no other commandment greater than these.

Mark 12:30-31 (ESV)

Prayer

Lord, relationships are hard work and sometimes leave me with unmet expectations and grief. I know that I need to relate to people, and you desire me to touch the lives you intersect with mine. I want to be available for you to use me to bless others. When I put myself in relationships that you never intended or avoid the ones you fully intend for me to engage in, forgive me and help me to be to others what you desire me to be. Too often, I give myself to the wrong people in the wrong ways and end up with emotional wounds. Help me to seek you first and connect appropriately to fulfill your reason for the relationship. I desire to be in my role in all relationships and to know when it is time to let go. Give me the wisdom I need to determine lifetime commitments and to nurture them in a healthy way. It is not about me; it is about the *Kingdom*.

Objectives

- Review the *discovery* exercises and note the outcomes.
- Discover your role in each of the relationships you are in.
- Resign to be in your role and allow the other person to be in his or her role (not easy, but necessary in order to have a healthy relationship).

DiSCOVERY

Relationship Inventory
(Reason/Season/Lifetime)

"A reason, a season, and a lifetime."

Author Unknown

People always come into your life for a reason, a season, and a lifetime. When you figure out which it is, you know exactly what to do.

When someone is in your life for a *reason*, it is usually to meet a need you have expressed outwardly or inwardly. They have come to assist you through a difficulty, or to provide you with guidance and support, to aid you physically, emotionally, or even spiritually. They may seem like a God-send to you, and they are. They are there for a reason; you need them to be.

Then, without any wrongdoing on your part or at an inconvenient time, this person will say or do something to bring the relationship to an end. Sometimes they die, Sometimes they just walk away. Sometimes they act up or out and force you to take a stand. What we must realize is that our need has been met, our desire fulfilled, their work is done. The prayer you sent up has been answered, and it is now time to move on.

When people come into your life for a *season*, it is because your turn has come to share, grow or learn. They may bring you an experience of peace or make you laugh. They may teach you something you have never done. They usually give you an unbelievable amount of joy. Believe it! It is real! But, only for a season. And like spring turns to summer and summer to fall, the season eventually ends.

Lifetime relationships teach you a lifetime of lessons; those things you must build upon in order to have a solid emotional foundation. Your job is to accept the lesson, love the person/people (anyway), and put what you have learned to use in all other relationships and areas in your life. It is said that love is blind, but friendship is clairvoyant. Thank you for being part of my life…

The Social Quest is where you assess all of your external relationships, i.e., parents, children, siblings, friends, etc. Why are they in your life? Are they for a specific "reason," only for a "season," or intended for a "lifetime"? Are you trying to hold on to relationships that have expired? Are you trying to control both sides of the relationship instead of allowing the other person to be in their role and you in yours? Are you in relationships that need to end or neglecting ones that need to be reconciled? Are you aware of relationships that you should start? You are only in control of what you say, what you do, or how you respond to what is said or done to you. Many times we give away the limited control we have to others, allowing them to control our thoughts and behaviors, our reactions, and responses. It is one thing to be influenced by others, but quite another to be controlled by them. At some point in your life, you have to assume control and responsibility for your life and be willing to "pay the cost to be the boss."

The Social Quest considers all of your horizontal relationships. That is all of the external relationships in your life. It might seem like a forgone conclusion that your family and loved ones are an automatic relationship and an easier relationship to work through. The assumption is that because you are family and love each other, things will automatically work themselves out. After all, you do not get to choose your relatives, only your friends. As I previously stated, every one of your relatives, except the person you choose to marry, is the result of someone else's decision. If you are from a culture that believes in arranged marriages, then you may not have even chosen your mate. You did not get to choose your parents, they chose each other, and you are the result of their choice. Unless you adopted your children, you did not get to choose them either; they are the result of an earlier decision you made to be intimate with another person. Even if you did adopt your child(ren), your ability to choose may have had some limits depending on the process used for the adoption. The point is, your parents, siblings, aunts, uncles, cousins, in-laws, and out-laws became your relatives because of a decision made by someone other than you. However, the quality of the relationship with each of these people is a decision that is partly yours. The other person also has a role in determining the quality of the relationship based on their participation.

To connect with people is to establish a rapport or relationship with them. It requires coming together, trusting, and sharing-mentally and emotionally. My husband, Michael, is a Licensed Marriage and Family Therapist (LMFT) and has theorized that open, effective communication invites transparency that encourages trust, and through trust, the relationship is affirmed. As human beings, we are instinctively wired to interact and connect with each other. However, connection in a relationship does not happen by chance. It has to be intentional. You reach out to a person; that person, in turn, reaches out to you. You open the lines of communication by sharing a little of yourself, and the other person responds in kind. The progressive exchange creates a connection. A value is placed on the connection and what follows is a relationship.

There is a bond in family relations that is often deeper than any other. Family relations are potentially "automatic" connections with people who are already in your circle of trust. I say potential because although you are related by blood, sometimes it is more difficult to relate and build trust with family than with strangers. How you relate to your family members can span a long emotional range from reasonably connected and loving to the extremely unhealthy place of being estranged. Trust typically happens automatically with babies and their parents, especially the mother. When a child is born, it is 100 percent dependent on someone to feed and care for him or her in order to survive. That person is typically the parent who birthed the child. We all know that there are those exceptions where the parent and person most responsible for the care of that child neglects or even abuses the child, and subsequently, the responsibility transfers to someone else. Even in cases of neglect and abuse, the child usually still trusts that person until he or she is cognitively advanced enough to learn that the person is untrustworthy. It is learned behavior. There is another unhealthy extreme, and in the counseling field, we call this being "enmeshed." This is when the two people are so connected that the relationship promotes unhealthy dependency and codependency. It is often seen in parent-child relationships when the child is unable to function independently because of the constant reliance on the parent, or the parent is unable to allow the child to become independent and is continually intruding in the life of the child. It creates an unhealthy dependency.

Even when the bond between a parent and a child is not enmeshed, it is often difficult for parents to shift from being the parent of a child with full authority over the decisions and relationships in their life to the parent of an adult and trade the authority for influence in the adult son or daughter's life. Likewise, it is equally difficult for the child to assume the responsibility for his or her decisions as an adult and release the parent from the consequences of them. There are no clear lines of embarkation into adulthood. Although the law has established an age when it will cease to consider a person as a child and hold them accountable as an adult, those laws are unable to determine maturity at a specific age.

The Social Quest is a point of decision. Parents can decide to allow their age-appropriate children to be adults with full responsibility and accountability for their decisions. You gave them life, but you cannot live it for them. At some point, you have to trust that you have taught them right from wrong, and they learned the lessons. Now they have to be permitted to demonstrate that they learned what you taught them by being able to make decisions without the constant interference of their parent(s). Let them live *"their"* lives by making decisions and experiencing the outcome. At those transitional times, allow them to occupy the position of authority that they have the maturity for; you take the position of influence. If you have nurtured a relationship of respect, it will be evident in the degree of influence you have in their adulthood. Your son or daughter will be confident and competent to make wise choices and to be the person of moral and noble character that you demonstrated for them.

Consider this visual reference for the transitional milestones in your parent-child relationship; when a child is young, inexperienced, and lacks the maturity to make decisions for his or her own safety and well-being, the parent should be in front of the child, leading and guiding. From that position, the parent is able to be a protector and shield the child from dangers by identifying pitfalls and hazards of life while being a role model of good, responsible decision-making. As the child demonstrates self-awareness and maturity, usually during late adolescence, the parent's position should shift side-by-side. From that position, the parent walks beside the child through this phase of life as a champion, allowing the child to have an unobstructed view of what he or she faces ahead, but the parent can still be a shield when needed. This phase allows for collaboration and negotiation about decisions, giving the child some experience with consequences and rewards associated with decision making. Finally, the transition through adolescence into adulthood should prompt the shift to position the child in front with a full, unobstructed view of the road ahead of him or her, and the parent's position is behind the child in more of a support posture. The parent now has more influence than authority. The parent is an encourager, advisor, and coach in the life of the child. If done right, the position of influence is more powerful than the one of authority. The child is now a young adult, fully capable of making his or her decisions, but also aware that you, the parent is still relationally behind him or her. From this position, the child may choose to consult with the parent and allowinfluence, support, or input. The parent is close enough to catch the child if he or she falls but can also be hands-off and observe the child's journey through life from the "back seat." That close proximity is the result of a relationship that has been well nurtured throughout the developmental transitions.

Parents have an obligation to know their role/position in their child's life. A parent that stays in front too long could create insecurity or an unhealthy dependency for the child and inhibit his or her responsible growth. Likewise, a parent that shifts too soon risks leaving the child ill-prepared for life and responsible decision-making. There is no specific age for these transitions. They are individual and circumstantial. However, the relational parent will get the cues through knowing the child and being engaged in his or her life. This becomes increasingly more difficult for divorced, non-custodial parents who only have limited scheduled opportunities to relate to their child(ren), also for single parents whose circumstances require them to be out of the home working or are otherwise absent out of necessity. In these cases, it is important to remember the value in quality versus quantity when it comes to the time you are able to relate with your child(ren). Lack of time may be a challenge but does not have to be an impossibility.

Now consider the parent/child relationship as an adult. The evidence of appropriately nurtured parent/child relationships during the formative years is revealed in healthy parent/child relationships in adulthood. Adults who are confident and comfortable were most likely prepared during childhood to engage in decisions responsibly. Conversely, when those transitions were not made, the results are grown. A woman who is still functioning like "daddy's little girl" as an adult is most likely struggling to be a wife who honors, respects, and puts her husband on the top shelf (under God, of course) of her life because her father is still occupying that place in her life. Similarly, the grown man who is "momma's boy" and finds himself running to his mother to seek her consultation in times when he should be extending that respect to his wife.

This is not to say that we should not go to our parents for advice or be respectful and considerate toward our parents. However, this is the reason Scripture instructs to "leave your mother and father and be united unto our spouse" (Ephesians 5:31, ESV). Honoring your spouse does not have to mean being dishonorable to your parents. Even if your parents refuse to transition, you *must*!

Siblings add another dimension to the Social Quest. As you consider your role and relationship with your sister(s) and/or brother(s), think about where you fit in the birth order in your family. There is a growing amount of research available to raise your awareness about how the position of your birth influences your character and way of relating to your siblings and others. It is interesting to note that every child born into a family is born into a different family than their siblings. The dynamics in the family with the arrival of the firstborn are certainly changed. With the first comes the excitement and newness of parenthood and all of the firsts that accompany it. All of the most idealistic goals, dreams, and nuances are put into motion. Nothing is too good for the new little one. Life, schedules, and perspectives are adjusted to accommodate the needs of this new addition to the family.

The new member of the family requires preplanning when doing even simple tasks. Before children, a parent or couple could just leave the house to run out to the store with no consideration for who will stay with the baby or if taking the baby, what added efforts would be required; car seat, stroller, diaper bag, bottle, etc. If you have been accustomed to being spontaneous and carefree, adding a child(ren) to your life will require adjustment. The firstborn, only child is subjected to the trial and error of the parents. S/He is precious cargo and can barely learn to walk because of the constant rescue of the new inexperienced parent. This level of constant care impacts the confidence, perspective, and ultimately the personality of the child.

By the time the second child arrives, another adjustment is imminent. Sometimes the novelty of a new baby may have worn off depending on the length of time between the births. Parenthood has become more of the norm than an adventure, and the need to go overboard may have subsided. Clearly, the relationship with child two is unintentionally different from the first. At the very least, the second child is not the center of everyone's attention because that attention has to be shared with the other child from the very beginning of life. Certainly, the age/maturity, socioeconomic state, and preparedness are factors. Each additional birth continues to shift the dynamics within the family and, therefore, creates a different environment within the home. Besides the individual personalities of each child, the climate of the home and the timing of each birth make a difference. The firstborn will always be the first and have the joy or surprise associated with being first. The subsequent child(ren) will have to contend with being next, behind the one in front of him or her, and will have the benefit or challenge of living in the older siblings' shadow. That could be a positive thing or a struggle depending on the child and the parent(s). If there is another child that follows, the second-born becomes the middle child. There is much research on the effects of being the middle child. Very often, the middle child has to process the fact that s/he is not the oldest or the youngest and often lives in a constant state of competition for attention. Again, depending on that child's temperament, it can be a positive or a challenge. Attention-seeking behaviors manifest in a variety of ways; overachiever, underachiever, behavior problems, or a great balance and peacekeeper of the family. It really depends greatly on the individual and also the way the parents or caregivers nurture that child in the overall family dynamic. Finally, the last born forever holds the spot of "baby of the family" and all that comes with that distinction.

For instance, I was raised as the youngest in a family

with two girls. My older sister was born to a sixteen-year-old unemployed, high school, single mother who still lived with her mother, who was also a single mother. I, on the other hand, was born to the same mother, but she was an eighteen-year-old married woman with a gainfully employed, loving husband. We were born to the same parent, but undoubtedly different families. Besides our varied personalities, our respective references for our family of origin impacted how we related to each other as sisters. It was relevant for me, when sorting out the issues in my own Social Quest, and determining my role in the relationship with my sister, to take into consideration our different perspectives and the fact that although born to the same mother, we were born into two very different family dynamics. Even though she was adopted by our father and had his last name, there seemed to always be something missing for her. I will not attempt to tell her story because only she can. What I will say is that from my observation, her life decisions, relationships with men, and ultimate outcomes appear to be connected to how she conceptualized her life and relationship with dad. Although I had nothing to do with my mother's decisions that resulted in when or how my sister and I were conceived, it most definitely played a role in the way my sister and I were socialized and subsequently related to each other. In my LifeQuest™ journey,

I dealt with my issues, and in the wisdom of my serenity, I changed the things I could by having the conversations I needed to have and speaking my truth. I also accepted the things I could not change by releasing the things that are not mine to change. As a result, I have a loving relationship with my older sister, and I give her myself fully and accept whatever she gives me of her. We sincerely love each other and are loving toward each other. I stay in my role and allow her to be in hers.

I am also the oldest sibling because my father's decisions in his life resulted in the birth of a daughter younger than me. Another sibling that I am related to, but I had no control over. It needs to be said that while my younger sister and I have our father in common, I did not grow up with her and therefore was not nurtured in my formative years as an older sister. I learned of her existence as an adult, and I had the benefit of maturity to assist me with the willful acceptance of this thing that I could not change. Initially, I was undeniably more excited to learn of her being my sister than she was learning of me being hers. Understandably, she had to process growing up her whole life believing someone else was her father. She had missed out on eighteen years of life with our father, and I had him from the beginning of my life. Again, my LifeQuest™ journey helped me to process my role in this sibling relationship and to explore the possibilities for an earnest relationship with my sister. Over time, she became willing, and we both assumed our respective roles as student and teacher and navigated the path to a mutually loving and respectful sisterly relationship that we maintain to this day.

I think it is interesting that in this current culture, having "friends" has taken on a whole new meaning. I also believe that some have become confused about what it truly means to be a "friend" and to have one. It is so much more than the number of names on your Facebook. The ability to nurture that number of people as "friends" is unrealistic and changes the perspective of what true friendship requires.

There are so many other social relationships to consider. Every person that touches your life makes a contribution. Some of them are large deposits that add obvious value; others are no less valuable because of the lessons learned from the hurtful or negative experience. Choose to honor the value of each kind of experience. Life has a way of providing second chances, giving you an opportunity to complete unresolved issues or to close a chapter in your life with the gift of a valuable lesson learned and the ability to move forward in growth. Your life will cross with many others in your lifetime, but beware; every crossing is not meant to yield a connection. For those that connect, determine your role in that relationship and seek to fulfill it. For those that do not, even if the person is your relative, be willing to create safe boundaries that allow you to love them in obedience to the Word of God while protecting yourself from the threat of abuse. It is not the will of God for you to be abused or mistreated by anyone, even your kin!

I recall hearing and making a note of this statement, "The success of relating to another depends 90 percent on you and 10 percent on the other person." I believe there is some truth in that philosophy. When you control yourself, your words, and actions, you have a powerful influence over the outcome of the interactions in the relationship. The fact is that you can never control the other person so just control what you can control—YOU. Your self-control should result in influence depending on the quality of the relationship. "Kindness is like heaping burning coals on the person's head" (Proverbs 25:22, NIV, and Romans 12:20, NIV). Society says the same thing in a different way, "Kill them with kindness."

I am reminded of a story in a devotional I read years ago entitled "The 60/60 Rule." The story is of a neighbor who learned a great relational lesson during a big snowstorm. The person was new to the neighborhood and became acquainted with his next-door neighbor while they were both shoveling snow following a snowstorm. The new neighbor noticed that the man next door was working faster than he. While he was still working on his driveway, the neighbor had finished with his own driveway and was working on the public sidewalk that ran in front of both their houses. As the neighbor continued on the sidewalk, the new neighbor noticed that the other man had shoveled well beyond his own property line and was now shoveling his sidewalk. By the time the new neighbor finished his driveway and started on the sidewalk just in front of his own house, he connected with the neighbor who was now also in front of his house. The new neighbor thanked him with astonishment and listened as the man told him about the 60/60 Rule. He said, "I learned a long time ago that if you operate under the 50/50 rule, meaning, you only do your part and I only do mine, neither of us doing any more than we have to, many things will fall between the cracks. When people shoot for the 50 percent mark, they may cut a few corners and unintentionally fall short… or purposely act a little stingy." He said I do 60 percent, ensuring an overlap so that nothing falls through the crack." He concluded by saying, "If we both do 60 percent, we can guarantee that nothing will fall through the crack."

How do you think that personal commitment to do more in that neighborly exchange contributed to the quality of that relationship? That man utilized his 90 percent influence, doing what he had control over (his actions) and ensured the success of that relationship. If you enter a relationship expecting the other person to fulfill your expectations, you set yourself up for disappointment and resentment. However, if you enter the relationship doing and giving what you can to it, the odds are in favor of the relationship being affirmed and esteemed. In the story, the neighbor said, "I do 60 percent." He never said, "I expect you to do 60 percent." His stated conclusion was that if both of them choose to do more, there are some guarantees. Keep in mind that the other neighbor always had the option to only do his share, 50 percent. Even if that is what he chose to do, the neighbor doing 60 percent has accounted for the overlap. What a great life lesson!

Reflection

As you have gone through life at each developmental stage, you have met new people from different walks of life. You may even have friends from grade school during your formative years that you still keep in touch with—tried and true. Conversely, some of those relationships from your youth were short-lived and did well to last for the brief school year that you shared temporarily. Still, others were acquaintances that you might have met as a result of your lives crossing because you were on the same little league team or in the same extra-curricular activity temporarily, but a little more significant. As you continue through life into adulthood, you have countless references for relationships that have come and gone, and the memories that were gained from those encounters are still with you.

I have shared this thought-provoking message about relationships for your consideration as you transverse the Social Quest. People always come into your life for a reason, a season, or a lifetime. When you figure out which it is, you are better prepared to deal with the state of the relationship.

The interesting thing to note is that while Jesus walked this earth and was the relational reason for multiple people, He surrounded Himself with a select few chosen people, and those men could fit in all three categories. Certainly, He was in their lives for a reason, but you can also note the reciprocal relationship that lasted for a season on earth with options for a lifetime relationship in eternity. I love this reference because since Christ is our example in life, particularly as it relates to relationships, there is a lesson to be learned about how we should consider our own relationships. Although He ministered to many, he retreated to a more intimate circle of friends that He specifically chose. They were not perfect, and most of them had habits and shortcomings that were appalling. He had a call, a purpose, and those men were part of it. Like you, Christ's relationships with His inner circle were complex and not always free from challenges, but He loved them and knew them and stayed in His role while allowing them to have their role in the relationship. There is so much more that could be said and comparisons that could be explored right here, but let's keep moving forward.

Sometimes, even relationships with people in our inner circle are toxic and threaten our emotional wellness. The relationship might even be with a parent, sibling, or loved one, but because of circumstances beyond your control, the relationship is not safe for you to continue. Abusive relationships are an example of this kind of relationship that may need to be distanced for your own safety. If you are in an unhealthy or unsafe relationship with someone, even if that person is a close relative, you are encouraged to consider your safety. I believe that the biblical instruction to "honor" our parents (Ephesians 6:2, NIV) is sometimes confused with the necessity to remain in a close relationship. It is possible and permissible to honor them from a safe distance. Note that the scripture does not place conditions on honoring them. It is not only if they earn or deserve to be honored. In fact, it gives consequences for *not* honoring them. This act of obedience is between you and God, more than you and your parents. It has an eternal consequence. You can honor them and satisfy the act of obedience from a physically or emotionally safe distance.

Now consider your own relationships and your role in them (to be the "*teacher* of *you*" and the "student of the other person"). Do an inventory of the relationships in your inner circle. Is the relationship a reason, a season, or a lifetime? Note the condition of those relationships and determine if there is something that you should and could do to improve the relationship? Are you willing to do it? This assignment will require much self-reflection and introspection. Don't rush through it. It may also require conversations with others.

Mother: _____

Father: _____

Other Parent: _____

Sibling: _____

Sibling: _____

Child: _____

Child: _____

Other Relative: _____

Other Relative: _____

Friend: _____

Friend: _____

Co-Worker: _____

Co-Worker: _____

Neighbor/Other: _____

Resolve

I acknowledge that I have a role to play in the lives of
the people I have a relationship with. I accept my role as I
complete the inventory of relationships in my life and make
the determination of status; reason, season, lifetime. I will
endeavor to do my part to nurture the lifetime relationships
in my life, contributing who I am and what I have to them.
I will be available and accessible to the relationships that
cross my life for a specific reason, making the contribution
required of me, and I will be open to receive from my sea-
sonal relationships the instruction and insight given and the
joy shared. I desire to cover the gap by giving 60 percent.
I will seek you, Lord, for clarity and guidance and vow to
trust you for the wisdom.

THE TRANSITIONAL QUESTS

Affirmation

"Step back in perspective, open your heart, and welcome transition into a new phase of life."

Linda Rawson

Scripture

"Therefore, if anyone is in Christ, he is a new creation; old things are passed away; behold, all things have become new."

2 Corinthians 5:17 (ESV)

Now that you have dealt with the relationships in your life and worked through how to move forward in them, knowing your role, let us proceed to transition in your life journey. It is important to recognize that transitions are places where you are required to make decisions about how to move forward. The Transitional Quests include the Emotional Quest and the Mental Quest. Each of these milestones will require deeper introspective processing. To aid in the process, there are two visual references that come to mind; a bridge and a bag. A bridge comes in many variations, but the commonality in them all is that they are necessary in order for the traveler to get from where s/he is to where s/he is trying to go, and if the bridge is on the path you are taking, you will need to cross it or be required to take an alternate route; one that may delay your progress.

The bridge is the obstacle that you face on your way to where you are going. For the person who is afraid of heights, this is a significant point of decision. I wonder what you are most afraid of; going up or falling down? How important is it to you to get to the other side? A detour means getting off course or even backtracking. Going forward means having to confront your fears, and conquer them. I live in central Florida, and crossing bridges often means the difference between getting to experience the splendor of some of the most beautiful beaches and breathtaking locations at the most southern end of the United States. Conversely, for the people who live in the most southern distances of the state, crossing the bridge could be the difference between getting to the safety of the higher ground or perishing in a storm because this is a hurricane territory. Sometimes you have to decide to take the bridge!

The other transitional reference is a bag. It is quite simply a container that can be used to transport objects more easily. The issue is not the bag; it is just the container. The issue is the contents. You are responsible for the items you put in your life bag, and you will have to carry the weight that those items add. When my girls were younger but old enough to walk, I came to realize that they needed to learn to carry their own weight; not just the physical weight of their bodies by walking, but also the added weight of the items they desired to carry with them. So I purchased these cute little backpacks, just their size. When we traveled or went places, if they wanted to take their toys, books, and things that they wanted to have with them, they had to carry them in their backpacks. Some may say this is cruel, but when you are the one carrying the weight of everyone else's stuff, you have to make some changes or surcome to the pressure of the weight you are carrying. Don't miss this important teachable moment right here… It is a point of decision!

Let us walk through the transitional journey of the Emotional Quest and the Mental Quest together. This process will focus on getting rid of the excess weight you are bearing and getting clear about what issues are yours to carry, and more importantly, how our Lord has uniquely equipped you with just what is needed to do what he has purposed you to do on this earth during the season of your life here. Jerimiah 29:11 (NIV) says, "He knows the plans He has for you," so if He knows those plans and wants to ensure that you fulfill them, He will have to reveal them to you. Undoubtedly, He is doing His part; you have to do your part to remove those things that are hindering or distracting you from knowing and doing what you are divinely purposed to do. "And we know that in all things God works for the good of those who love Him, who have been called according to His purpose" (Romans 8:28, NIV).

EMOTIONAL QUEST

Affirmation

"I cannot change another person by direct action; I can only change myself! Others have the tendency to change in reaction to my change."

Unknown

Scripture

"Be kind and compassionate to one another, for-giving each other, just as in Christ God forgave you."

Ephesians 4:32 (NIV)

Prayer

God, grant me the serenity to accept the things I cannot change, the courage to change the things I can, and the wisdom to know the difference. Living one day at a time; enjoying one moment at a time; accepting hardship as a pathway to peace; taking, as Jesus did, the sinful world as it is, not as I would have it; trusting that you will make all things right so that I may be reasonably content in this life and supremely joyous with You forever in the next. Amen.

On life's journey, there are some straight roads, winding roads, and bumpy roads. There are some shortcuts, detours, and dead ends. Along the way, there are road signs, mile markers, and rest areas that will allow you to get instructions, recalibrate, and ensure you are still on the intended course. You are encouraged to pay attention to, and take the breaks intended to reset your mind, will, emotions and increase your stamina for the remainder of the journey. This transition from the work you have done with relationships is a definite shift in focus. Now that you know how to be a student, learning from others as you relate with them, and a teacher, better able and willing to take ownership for your role and responsibilities, you are better prepared for the work that lies ahead. The journey has been long and deep thus far, and you are still here.

You are now at the place in your progress where you are ready to take the bridge and ascend up and over the many hurdles or obstacles that have stalled or inhibited your progress. It will be necessary for you to lighten your load and drop the extra burden of weight that is slowing you down, preventing you from making progress, or threatening to thwart your trip altogether. The Emotional Quest will require you to deal with your baggage so that you may continue the journey lighter and more able to move forward, uninhibited by extra weight.

Objectives

- To become aware of emotional baggage and the weight it causes—inhibiting my ability to move forward effectively in the journey of life.
- To identify the baggage and determine to whom it belongs; me, someone else, or God; and to make a decision about what to do with it.
- To take actions to free myself with God's help of the emotional baggage that has been holding me back and delaying my progress.
- Transition over the bridge of life into my divine purpose.

The Emotional Quest is the milestone in your journey where you get to consider all of the "stuff" you have been carrying through life and what purpose it is serving for you. You will assess all of the experiences and things that were both controllable and uncontrollable and the impact they have left on your life. Do you need them for the remainder of your journey, or is this a good time to drop some weight? In the Emotional Quest, you will inventory your life to get rid of the excess baggage that is just clutter in your life. It is time to sort through the issues of your life to determine what to "save," "unload," "deal-with," or "surrender to God." In keeping with the idea of "cleaning" out, I call these the SUDS.

We all have issues that we have carried around for years with no resolve or surrender. Some of your life experiences, both negative and positive, have taught you valuable lessons and have actually been a catalyst for growth. Those valued experiences are the ones worth holding onto (save) for future reference, even the hurtful ones that taught you what not to do. For instance, if you were in a marriage that ended in divorce. You, like most people, would want to write off the situation and all of the misery with the signing of the divorce decree. Let me encourage you to reconsider. Surely there are some things of value worth remembering, even if only what not to do in the future. Sometimes we are too quick to discard important lessons, considering them "the past."

It is possible that some of them are things that you have made your issue(s) but have no ability to change. They are not your issues. In fact, they are just burdens that are hindering you from having peace. Those are the issues that should be returned (unloaded) to the person or persons who have responsibility for them. When I say return to the rightful owner, I mean allow other people's issues to be their issues, not yours. Work on minding your own business and leaving other's business alone. An indicator of whether you are the rightful owner is if you have the ability to control the outcome of the issue. If you do not, then you are not the owner, and it is not your issue (even if you are impacted by it). For instance, you may be married to someone who has an addiction. Obviously, the addiction affects your life because you love the person, are married, and want your spouse to be free from the addiction. However, you do not have the ability to control the person who is addicted or deliver him/her from it. The addicted person has to make the change. Therefore, the issue belongs to the addicted spouse, and you should allow him/her to deal with/resolve it. The person who has control over the outcome owns it. In a situation like this, your issue might be that your spouse is not taking care of the issue, and it is disrupting the whole household. In this case, your issue is not the addiction because you can't change that. The issue is the disruption of your life and the child(rens). You are a point of decision. What will you do about the disruption and the unhealthy environment?

You could choose to (deal with it), seek counsel for the effects this situation is having on you and the family. You could choose to leave the situation for the safety and well-being of the family or any number of other options unique to your personal situation. Another option is to (surrender) it to the Lord and let Him deal with it. It is not helpful to you or your spouse for you to carry around the burden of his/her addiction. It usually results in you becoming co-dependent and an enabler that allows the addicted person to continue in addiction instead of getting delivered from it. This also applies to other issues that are not yours.

As a counselor, I have knowledge of the common occurrence of people carrying the weight of the issues of their past, both traumas and dramas, that have just been ignored or suppressed but not dealt with or overcome. The error that is often made is looking for someone else to make you feel good about yourself. Jumping in and out of relationships believing the person and/or the relationship will be the answer to the emptiness or emotional pain you feel. This is a dangerous act because neither the relationship nor the person is enough to overcome the hurts of what happened to you in childhood caused by someone else. I saw a quote that says it perfectly, "Relationships don't heal childhood wounds...It highlights them" (Beverly Adre).

I see so many women and men in search of *"The One,"* but how can you truly love another when you are still trying to figure out what love is for yourself? How can you be prepared to relate in a healthy way with someone else when you are still bitter about the way you were treated in the last relationship? More importantly,

It would be nice if we could change people because if we could, I know several parents who would sign up for the ability to change their children, especially during the pivotal transitional stages of development, i.e., sleepless infancy, "terrible twos," and trying teenage years. As parents, we have our own ideals as it relates to our children. Some of us have planned out their lives before they are even able to walk or talk. It is a great thing in our minds to see them all grown up and successful (according to our definition of success), but when they are grown and have their own plans and definition for success, and how their life should look, the power struggle begins. The truth is that we are not in control and cannot, no matter how hard we try, change them. Remember, the Social Quest, we have influence if we have handled our relationship with our child(ren) well. Influence is almost as powerful as control.

If the issue you are working through belongs to someone that you have already dealt with relationally in the Sexual or Social Quest and decided that the relationship is not healthy for you to continue in, it may not be feasible to have a conversation about this outstanding issue with that person. Especially if that person is someone that you have already eliminated or put in a limited access status in your life. In the case of a person who has hurt you or does not handle your emotional well-being responsibly and respectfully, both the person and the issue should simply be surrendered to the Lord and move on. Additionally, for that person, you can process the issue for yourself and, through the process of your own self-awareness, get to a place of closure without actually having a conversation with the person.

On the other hand, if this person is someone you intend to continue in a relationship with, or you need to figure out how to have an amicable connection with because of circumstances, i.e., co-parenting with someone you have divorced or decided not to marry, a solution-focused conversation may be necessary. No need to go in search of more issues to take on; most certainly, yours should be more than enough.

As a mother, I can remember having a "mommy purse." It was the collection point for everyone's stuff. If you are a mother, you may be able to relate to this analogy. The "mommy purse" is the purse that the mommy carries but somehow becomes the depository for the kid's toys, diapers, half-eaten snacks, extra clothes, one shoe, etc. It doesn't stop with just the kid's belongings, but it also has the extra items that dad couldn't fit in his pockets and the thing that belongs to the friend or co-worker that had not gotten around to be returning yet. Truthfully, some days, I couldn't even remember what was in my purse or how it got there. Eventually, it would become so heavy; I had to stop and clean it out so that I could continue to carry it without injuring myself from the weight.

During the cleaning out process, I would discover that I had accumulated these snacks, toys, and all kinds of things that belonged to my kids, my husband, and others because I was willing to take their things and carry them when they were unwilling. The weight of all of those things caused me discomfort and even pain, but the rightful owner was free from the burden of the weight. They were no longer even concerned about the items because I had them, and they were now my issue. They also did not have the responsibility of carrying them around because I was doing that for them. I continued to carry them around, occupying space in my purse that could be better utilized by useful things that served a purpose or removed to just lighten my load.

When I stopped and sorted through all of the "stuff," returned the toys, snacks, etc., to the rightful owners, paid the bills, filed the receipts, and discarded the trash, my purse returned to a manageable weight, and the resulting discomfort ceased. The Emotional Quest is a point of decision about the excess emotional weight you are carrying through life that may be hindering your progress, causing discomfort, or preventing you from being available for the purpose God intends for your life.

Like the additional baggage in the "mommy purse," our lives become cluttered with extra items that require the occasional purging. Some of the items are known but ignored; others are unknown because they were added to our lives during challenging circumstances when we were distracted or less attentive. In either case, there are issues and perhaps people that you have been carrying around with you that really are not yours to carry and may be more of a hindrance than a help. People should have already been eliminated or put in a "limited access" status during your Social Quest, but just in case someone slid by your process of elimination, here is another opportunity. Additionally, there are some things, not people, that have just been clutter or waste in your life and should be disposed of because they are not doing you or anyone else any good. Those things have no real value and, in fact, may be inhibiting your progress; get rid of the weight they cause so you may travel lighter. On the other hand, there are some things that are lessons learned and will serve as valuable references for you in the future, restore those experiences, references, and people to your life, and gain the benefit of the value they offer.

I am reminded of a show that came on television called *Clean Sweep*. The show took a team of people to the homes of families who needed some assistance with sorting through the accumulation of things in their home, causing the items that matter the most to them to be lost in the clutter. The host of the show often had to help the families through their emotions about the loss of some things by helping them determine the value of the item. This show is a very real and visual reference for what sometimes happens to us with issues of life. We have such an accumulation of issues that we are not sure what is significant and should be kept or what should be discarded. We have become emotional hoarders! LifeQuest™ has come to help you with the emotional sorting to determine what you should "save," "unload," "discard," or "surrender" to God. You are at a point of decision. Let the sorting begin.

Reflection

There is wisdom in packing light when you are going on a trip and will have to manage all of the bags you bring on the journey, especially if you will have to carry them and bear their weight. Consider the events of your life that have caused you negative emotions, i.e., disappointment, hurt, betrayal, grief, and even anger. Don't forget the losses, i.e., relationships, deaths, promises, and dreams. What is the status of those events, resolved or unresolved? For the ones that are unresolved, are they helping or hindering you from moving forward in life?

Remember, not all emotional issues are created equally. There are some issues that positively add value to your journey and serve as an affirming reference for your growth. Those issues undoubtedly should be in the *"save"* column. Others may be categorized as negative but are valuable life lessons that serve as a valued reminder or point of reference for future decisions. Place those in the *"save"* column as well.

The life events that affect you but truly are not within your control to change should be *"unloaded."* The issue may be a result of you hanging on longer than feasible, or maybe a refusal to accept that a relationship is over, or maybe your failure to realize that you were a victim and not at fault. Regardless, the issue belongs to someone other than you and needs to be removed from your emotional bag.

Avoiding issues has the ability to breed stress. Some matters need to be addressed and resolved without delay. I like to say it this way; you have to allow yourself to *feel* the emotion—so that you can *deal* with the issue—so that you can *heal* from the pain. It is a process, but the more important thing is that you have the power to change the outcome for your issues. It may require the courage to have a conversation with someone and speak your truth to someone. If a conversation is not enough, confrontation may be more suitable to reach a resolution. I appreciate Dale Carnegie's reference for confrontation that includes care for the individual—Carefronting. Remember, you have the ability to change the outcome because you own the issue and control your thoughts, words, and actions associated with it.

Finally, there are experiences and circumstances that have either been beyond your control or your direct decisions that have caused you great emotion, but it is just more than you can handle. The issue has no useful value or purpose in your life and would be best as a decision to "*surrender*" to God through prayer and possibly through forgiveness. So much of the emotional weight we carry is due to hurts from our past, and we have been holding onto them instead of taking them to the Lord. The Scripture says, "His yoke is easy and His burden is light" (Matthew 11:30, NIV). If the burdens you are bearing are heavy, lighten your load by giving it to the Lord through prayer. Remember that forgiveness does not mean that you absolve the person of the wrong or that you have forgotten the hurt or that what was done was okay; it just means you will no longer allow it to weigh you down or keep you from living your life the way you choose. Forgiveness frees you from the weight of the burden and lifts you above the situation.

The table below provides a place for you to unpack your emotional baggage and annotate the final disposition. It is important to note an expected time for the action you will take as a record of accountability. Before you begin, there is a video skit and script entitled "Baggage" on www. skitguys.com that provides a great representation of carrying baggage through life. There is both a male and a female version. Watch the video or read it before you do the reflective exercise.

Now that you have the visual reference for what it looks like to carry your baggage through life, you are ready for the exercise. In the chart below, list the things you would identify as emotional baggage, consider what action you should take using the SUDS references, and determine what final disposition is appropriate.

For instance, if you are a single parent who is struggling with maintaining balance in the co-parenting arrangement you have made with the other parent, the chart might have the following annotations: Issue: Shared parenting time, Action: Deal/Unload, Disposition: Conversation with (name) to communicate expectations, concessions, and consequences; then Unload. Ultimately, you cannot change the other person or make him/her adhere to any agreed-upon arrangement. However, once there is agreement on the expectations, failure on his/her part to honor the agreement should be met with appropriate consequences. It is not your responsibility to manage that parent's relationship with his/her child(ren). If the relationship becomes estranged or otherwise hindered, that parent owns the control to restore or repair it. Likewise, if the relationship is not restored or repaired, that parent also has to live with the consequences. You are probably thinking, "but what about the child(ren) that suffers?" The truth is, you carrying the burden for that relationship by always adjusting your plans, making excuses or concessions for the other parent's failure to honor his/her responsibility for parenthood does not guarantee a healthy relationship for the child with that parent. Instead, you have likely started an unhealthy pattern of enabling behavior and set up a formula for resentment and bitterness within yourself that eventually becomes baggage and weight that inhibits your forward movement in that relationship and, potentially, in life. Finally, note whether the issue was resolved or ongoing. Resolution is about the issue no longer being emotional baggage for you. In the scenario provided, even if the other parent continues to be unreliable or inconsistent with co-parenting responsibilities, you have made the issue his/hers, not yours. If s/he is canceling at the last minute, for whatever reason, let him/her tell the child(ren) that s/he is not coming and why. You do not have to be the bearer of the let-down. You have established clear expectations and consequences for unmet expectations, and you no longer allow that parent's failures to impede your progress. Keep in mind, the effects on the child(ren) may be something that you will have to address, and you may even need to get professional counsel for them, but that is a different issue. Be careful not to confuse the two.

SUDS: Unpacking your Emotional Baggage

ISSUE/EVENT	ACTION (SUDS)	DISPOSITION

Issue/Event: An experience or decision that caused an emotional reference in your life, i.e., relationship, loss, disappointment.

Action—Save: Issues that maintain some value for your life and should be kept.

Action—Unload: Issues that belong to someone else because they are beyond your control to change.

Action—Deal: Issues that require action (conversation, confrontation/carefrontation, revelation) by you in order to resolve. You have the control to change the outcome.

Action—Surrender: Issues that have no value serve no helpful purpose in your life. Let go and let God handle it (forgiveness).

Disposition: What appropriate action did you take in order to complete your action (SUDS)? Who was involved? Was it resolved? How?

With the sorting accomplished, decide how you want to handle the issue(s) that you need to deal with. You may want to have a conversation with yourself or another person to address the issue in order to find a resolution. It is recommended regardless of who owns the issue, as demonstrated in the scenario I presented above. I suggest the conversation start with you processing your own perspective first before taking it to the other person. Take time to consider what thoughts, emotions, and references are happening internally that are shaping your opinions and beliefs about the situation. One way to process an issue in preparation for a conversation is to use a format common for problem-solving; problem/situation, action, result (PAR/SAR).

Be sure to clearly identify the issue/problem/situation and provide the context that will help the other person understand the reference that has led to the matter at hand. It is always a good idea to use personal identifying statements, i.e., my issue is… I have a problem with… so that you are speaking from your truth, based on what you have experienced, not making an accusation. When you speak to someone with a series of statements beginning with "you," it is like pointing your finger at someone when you are speaking to them; "you did not do what you said, "you always say you will, and then you don't." This is a definite setup for a defensive reaction.

The "Action" in PAR is reporting on one's own behavior: it is most accurate to reflect on how you have responded to this problem already. It obviously did not work, so you need to consider what other alternative actions might be feasible. A common definition of insanity is to keep doing the same thing and expect a different outcome. Clearly, if you want a different outcome, you will need to do something different. How are you presently handling this issue? Perhaps you were trying different things in hopes of a resolution, and now, out of frustration or defeat, you are not doing anything. Most assuredly, the issue will continue, and you will not reach your desired "Result" without action. Scripture says that even "faith without works is dead" (James 2:17, KJV). If your desire is to resolve the issue and eliminate the emotional baggage associated with it, action is necessary. Particularly if you are the owner of the issue, you will need to consider what future solution-focused action you will take, different from what has already been tried. How invested are you in the resolution? The next effort may require sacrifice, an act of selflessness, or a humble submission; forgiveness.

Emotions are an important part of the process and the conversation, but they should not lead the conversation. It is necessary to have a pleasant disposition and attitude and to be in a state of calm. Emotions can be such heavy-weights, keeping you down in the same despair you have struggled with for an extended period of time or can be used as an elevating springboard, lifting your up from that despair into a place of hope. Remarkably, the choice belongs to you.

Be honest about your emotions, and don't stuff them because they are sure to resurface sooner or later. It is best to present them when you are able to effectively reg-ulate them. Keep in mind that they are your inner feelings, not your thoughts or assumptions about the situation. They are very basic; fear, anger, joy, disappointment, frustration, etc. Too often, emotions and thoughts are confused when communicating. Thoughts are often wrongly communicated as feelings, i.e., "I feel like you are manipulating me!" More accurately stated, "I am confused by your inconsistent actions; therefore, I believe you are manipulating me, and it makes me sad." Identifying the emotion(s) should come first, then the thoughts or beliefs that contribute to those feelings. You could even follow up with another emotion for effect. You have clearly stated that you are confused and sad. These are your feelings/emotions. These emotions were caused by your thought/belief that the person is manipulating you by his/her inconsistent actions. If you are not clear about your own emotions, neither will the other person. Remember those feeling charts with different facial expressions that represent each emotion? It might be helpful to refer to one as a reference during this time because it is sometimes difficult to pinpoint what emotion most accurately represents how you truly feel.

Actually, your thoughts could be off base or an assumption instead of a fact, but your feelings are undeniable and should be shared and validated. Manipulation may not have been the intention of the other person, only your assumption based on the inconsistent actions. It is possible that there is some other reasonable explanation for the person's inconsistencies. Without the conversation and the opportunity to explanation and gain understanding, you would continue being emotional about what you think is going on, in error. Avoiding something does not make it go away; it only prolongs the inevitable. Misunderstandings account for 90 percent of all conflicts in relationships.

Allow for the possibility that the issue is a result of a

misunderstanding. Misunderstandings include ineffective communication, uncommunicated or unmet expectations, and a whole list of behaviors that involve jumping to conclusions without clarification or verification. It is your responsibility to request what you want or expect and verify that the other person clearly understands the request. It is not until you have that verification that you can safely expect to receive what you have asked for.

The Holy Scripture states that three things will last forever, "Faith, hope, and love, and the greatest of these is love" (1 Corinthians 13:13, NLT). If you choose to agree that the greatest is, in fact, love, stop to consider what that actually means. Faith is the basis of many spiritual belief systems, including Christianity. Without it, the entire theology would be null. Without faith, pleasing God becomes an impossibility (Hebrews 11:6, KJV). Just having it is not enough; it has to be activated and working (James 2:17, KJV). Faith, being the essence of things hoped for and evidence of things not yet manifested, is a requisite for hope (Hebrews 11:1, KJV). Some would uphold faith as an institution, yet it is inferior to love.

For many, hope is the fuel that keeps them going. Without it, their fate would be defeat, not just in some things, but in life as a whole. Scripture instructs those who believe in having hope in order to have the strength of heart

(Proverbs 13:12, NKJV). It is a consequence of mercy. Hope should not be deferred; it is the main ingredient for being blessed. Divine guidance is to believe in hope, even against hope (Romans 4:18, ESV).

Before there was faith, there was love because love paid the ultimate sacrifice even before faith existed. When there was no hope because Christ was crucified and it was thought that all hope was lost, love got up out of the grave and lived so that we could live. Love never fails! For this reason, we should "above all, love each other deeply, because love covers a multitude of sins" (1 Peter 4:8, NIV). Love truly is the greatest of all!

Please note that some of the issues you may have identified could require the assistance of a professional to help you process and resolve. If any milestone in LifeQuest™ reveals issues that are beyond your ability to overcome, please seek professional help. Take time now to identify a list of Behavioral Health resources and contact information where you may seek help.

Sources for Counseling Support
www.AMaysingCounseling.com
Insurance or EAP_____
Local Church _____

Center/Behavioral Health Clinic

College or University Behavioral Health Clinic

Internet/Directory

American Association of Christian Counselors:

www.aacc.net

American Counseling Association:

www.counseling.org

American Psychological Association:

www.apa.org

American Association of Marriage and Family Therapists:

www.aamft.org

National Board for Certified Counselors:

www.nbcc.org

Resolve

I choose to let go of the past and the hurtful memories it holds.

I choose to embrace the future and the new experiences that await me.

I choose to allow myself the possibility of a different experience, free from the shadows of the old.

I acknowledge that my parent(s) did the best they knew how in my childhood, and as an adult, I accept responsibility for my future without carrying the weight of their issues.

I believe that my past does not have to dictate my future; it's my choice!

I forgive my parents, I forgive my past offenders, and I forgive myself.

I open my mind and my heart to give and receive love.

I will use the value of the lessons learned and seek awareness and knowledge to use for future better choices and decisions.

I will reach out to my known resources for support and help.

MENTAL QUEST

Affirmation

"I am the master of my fate: I am the captain of my soul."

William Ernest Henly

Scripture

"Trust in the LORD with all your heart and lean not on your own understanding; in all your ways submit to him, and he will make your paths straight."

Proverbs 3:5-6 (NIV)

Prayer

Lord, I accept that I have been a student first and then a teacher. I have acquired references about who I am and how you have wonderfully made me with gifts, talents, knowledge, skills, and abilities that are specifically in preparation for how you intend to use me in the Kingdom. Now I need to have clarity about my place and my role in the business of the Kingdom. I realize that you have a plan for my life, and you desire that I know that plan so that I may fulfill it. Make your plans for me clear. Show me how to take what you have given me and use it for your glory. Identify the specific population, if there is one that you would have me touch. Increase my awareness and alertness about opportunities paid and charitable that will allow me to be in my purpose. I will always give you the glory! Amen.

Objectives

- To understand how God uniquely designed and created you for a specific purpose.
- To compile all of the information and revelations acquired through reflection and discovery exercises during the journey and reference them for confirmation or determination about your purpose call.
- To accept the call and, with prayerful consideration, establish a place of embarkation to align your life with your purpose.

DISCOVERY

The Mental Quest is about knowing what you need to know in order to do what you are called to do. Consider all of the self-awareness that you have already acquired and what it indicates; your purpose. Are you aware of a particular instance in your life when your experience was so significant that it has become part of your story (testimony)? Perhaps it is that incident that God allowed in your life in order to prepare you for what He has purposed for your life's mission. Do you remember a hurt, diagnosis, loss, or victimization? What about a special person, (s)hero, life-changer? Is there a situation that you are aware of that really touched your heart or broke your heart? Is there a certain population of people that you are drawn to? Now consider the gifts, talents, special personality, and all of the other things that you have come to realize about yourself that would qualify you for your purpose.

The discovery activities that you have been doing throughout this journey have perhaps revealed some information that you did not know or was not considered as preparation for your call because you were so focused on the skills you possess that qualify you for your job or your profession. Maybe you have believed that you volunteer to serve underprivileged communities because you are just a caring person, or that you became a *big brother* or *big sister* because you just like kids. It is possible for you to be working on a job or in a profession that you are getting paid to do and that utilizes the God-given gifts that are meant for the fulfillment of your calling. However, it is important for you to understand that "your purpose is not your job, it is your calling"—Beatrice Berry. I have heard it said that those things that produce the most emotion for you are your passion and what you would be most driven to impact; that thing that makes you cry or causes your blood to boil. It may be about advocacy, lawmaking, or amending the laws that were made. It may require an "aha" moment or even a movement to get inspired and motivated to action. Remember to make a decision to act. The call on your life is sure to manifest in your life when you seek God for the revelation of it.

The self-assurance needs to accept and walk in your call is, in part, the responsibility of God. The other part, however, is yours. You have to believe and receive it, knowing that you are not alone and God is always with you, ensuring that you have what you need to accomplish the mission before you. Regardless of your level of education, knowledge, skills, or abilities, it is God who has called you ad He who will equip you for this purpose. It will require you to be confident and to know who you are and whose you are.

If you have ever taken a psychology class, you have likely heard of the Hierarchy of Needs by Abraham Maslow. Psychologist Abraham Maslow first introduced his concept of a hierarchy of needs in his 1943 paper *A Theory of Human Motivation* and his subsequent book, *Motivation and Personality*. This hierarchy suggests that people are motivated to fulfill basic needs before moving on to other higher-level needs.

While there is some controversy about the theory, it provides a respected reference for the climb to self-actualization. Maslow's pyramid, referenced below, is the basis for the theory.

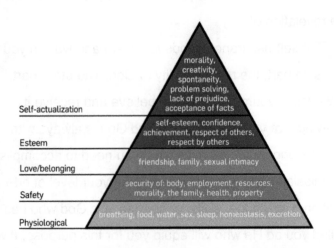

Maslow's Hierarchy of Needs

The lowest levels of the pyramid are made up of the most basic needs, while the more complex needs are located at the top of the pyramid. Needs at the bottom of the pyramid are basic physical requirements, including the need for food, water, sleep, and warmth. Once these lower-level needs have been met, you can move on to the next level of needs, which are for safety and security. As you progress up the pyramid, your needs become increasingly more psychological and social. Soon, the need for love, friendship, and intimacy become important. Further up the pyramid, the need for personal esteem and feelings of accomplishment take priority—the order matters.

There are five different levels in Maslow's Hierarchy of needs:

1. Physiological Needs

Includes the most basic needs that are vital to survival, such as the need for water, air, food, and sleep. Maslow believed that these needs are the most basic and instinctive needs in the hierarchy because all needs become secondary until these physiological needs are met. As believers performing the ministry of missions, we realize that it is counter-productive to try to minister salvation to someone who is hungry or without shelter. The person's focus will be more on the growling of his/her stomach than what you are saying. After all, how can a person realize the *love* of a *God* who allows him/her to be hungry? Besides the obvious display of humanity, it is why we feed the hungry before trying to lead them to Christ.

2. Security Needs

Includes need for safety and security. Security needs are important for survival, but they are not as demanding as physiological needs. Examples of security needs include a desire for steady employment, health insurance, safe neighborhoods, and shelter from the environment. The powerful emotions of fear, anger, and anxiety are often present when individuals lack in some of these very basic needs. These emotions are most often secondary to other more primal emotions such as insecurity, hopelessness, or hopelessness. What manifests is fear that develops into decisions and behaviors that are often harmful to the individual and sometimes others. I am reminded of the movie *Pursuit of Happiness* with Will Smith and his son, Jaden, portraying a businessman who lost his job and became homeless. His lack of shelter and stable employment caused him to act out in ways that were uncharacteristic of him, but he was afraid for the safety of his son and himself. Likewise, the movie *John Q,* played by Denzel Washington as a father who holds patients and doctors hostage in a hospital emergency room while demanding the hospital approve his son to be on the organ donor list for a heart transplant. His insurance was inferior for the medical care his son needed, and he feared for his son's life. He acted out of his helplessness that was manifested as fear and anger.

3. Social Needs

Includes need for belonging, love, and affection. Maslow considered these needs to be less basic than physiological and security needs. Relationships such as friendships, romantic attachments, and families help fulfill this need for companionship and acceptance, as does involvement in social, community, or religious groups. Believe it or not, God requires us to be connected socially to others. It is not His will for us to be secluded from others. He said, in Scripture, we should "not forsake assembling of ourselves together" (Hebrews 10:25, KJV). This is another reason why it is so important that you complete the work in the Social Quest and make it a part of your routine personal work. It matters whom you surround yourself with. It also matters who you are listening to and receiving from. God made us to need each other and the benefit that comes from being with others. We make each other the best versions of ourselves through our encouragement and challenge.

4. Esteem Needs

After the first three needs have been satisfied, esteem needs become increasingly more important. These include the need for things that reflect on self-esteem, personal worth, social recognition, and accomplishment. This is another indicator of the work you have done in the relational quests because we are typically esteemed through others first and what others think and say about us influences how we think of ourselves. This is why it is so important to consider the sources of our impressions. Just because your parents gave birth or contributed seed to create you does not automatically make them the credible source for your perspective of who you are or to determine your value and worth. Consider the Source!

5. Self-Actualizing Needs

The highest level of Maslow's hierarchy of needs. Self-actualized people are self-aware, concerned with personal growth, less concerned with the opinions of others and interested in fulfilling their potential and purpose. Self-actualized people have done the work to determine their social position. The ability for a person to reach the state of self-actualization when their physiological, social, security, and esteem needs are not met is extremely unlikely in the natural, scientific concepts. However, "nothing is impossible with God" (Luke 1:37, NLT).

Although there is still more to discovery and the journey is not over, the Mental Quest is where you begin to put things together mentally to first discover, then believe, then receive, and finally, accept God's divine call on your life. For this reason, you will begin the discovery exercise of the Spiritual Resume to create a single document that outlines each component of new information you have acquired during your LifeQuest™ and the knowledge that you were aware of before. The document should be formatted like a traditional resume for employment. Imagine you are applying for a position to fulfill your divine call. Your Spiritual Resume should reflect your noteworthy Accomplishments, Characteristics, and Attributes, Knowledge, Skills, and Abilities (KSA) that would qualify you for the position. Suggested Headings: *purpose, summary* of *qualifications, background, relevant experiences, major accomplishments/ testimony,* and *references.*

Purpose: To fulfill the call of God using the gifts, talents, knowledge, skills, and abilities He has equipped me with for the sake of the Kingdom. In the *summary of qualifications*: State the outcomes of all of the Discovery exercises you have completed, i.e., Spiritual Gifts Assessment, True Colors, and Five Love Languages. When writing your *background:* Note the things you know about your family of origin, your family's/your spiritual beliefs, your birth order, and any other remarkable information. *Relevant Experiences*: Those life experiences that taught you lessons worth "saving," the issues that you grew through, etc. *Major Accomplishments/Testimony*: Your story; the things that God has allowed you to go through in your life, and you came through it *victorious*, "more than a Conqueror through Him who loved us" (Romans 8:37, NIV). This is also the place to note the issues you have resolved in the reclamation of your life. Finally, your *references:* The people in your life who are your spiritual accountability partners, your "reason" and "lifetime" people, and those who have sown into your life and walked alongside you in this journey. These people may have prayed for you, counseled you, put you down so that you would have to learn to stand on your own; you know the ones.

This "Spiritual" resume will help you to focus on what you know that is relevant to you being able to do what you have been called to do. It is an essential part of the process because you must first know (believe) before you do (take action). Proverbs 23:7 (NIV) says, "For as he thinks in his heart, so is he." It is all relevant to becoming self-aware, self-actualized, and self-assured so that you will be able to walk out of your purpose! Just like "professional" resumes, this one is a living document that will need to be updated occasionally as you gain new experience and acquire more information worth documenting as a reference. You have only just begun. Now let us continue moving forward.

Spiritual Resume

Contact Information

Full Name

_____

Purpose

_____

_____

Summary of Qualifications

_____

_____

Background

_____

_____

Relevant Experience

_____

_____

Major Accomplishments/Testimony

_____

_____

References

_____

_____

Reflection

Mental Quest: "For as he thinks in his heart, so is he…"

Proverbs 23:7a (NKJV)

"Therefore, if anyone is in Christ, he is a new creation; the old has gone, the new has come!"

2 Corinthians 5:17 (ESV)

"…we have the mind of Christ."

1 Corinthians 2:16b (NKJV)

"I can do everything through Him who gives me strength."

Philippians 4:13 (NIV)

"For everyone born of God overcomes the world. This is the victory that has overcome the world, even our faith."

1 John 5:5

Now therefore fear the LORD, and serve him in sincerity and in truth: and put away the gods which your fathers served on the other side of the flood, and in Egypt; and serve ye the LORD. And if it seem evil unto you to serve the LORD, choose you this day whom ye will serve; whether the gods which your fathers served that were on the other side of the flood, or the gods of the Amorites, in whose land ye dwell: but as for me and my house, we will serve the LORD.

Joshua 24:14-15

"But I trust in your unfailing love; my heart rejoices in your salvation."

Psalm 13:5 (NIV)

"The thief comes only to steal and kill and destroy; I came that they may have life, and have it abundantly."

John 10:10 (ESV)

The Spirit of the Lord is on me, because He has anointed me to proclaim good news to the poor. He has sent me to proclaim freedom for the prisoners and recovery of sight for the blind, and to set the oppressed free.

Luke 4:18 (NIV)

"Teach me your way, LORD, that I may rely on your faithfulness; give me an undivided heart, that I may fear your name."

Psalm 86:11 (NIV)

The psalmist prays for an "undivided heart." Examine your own heart. Is it divided? What does that mean to you, and how does it impact your walk with God?

"Consequently, faith comes from hearing the message, and the message is heard through the word about Christ."

Romans 10:17 (NIV)

How does the Word of God impact the strength of your faith?

Read Romans 12:9-15 (NIV).

"Press toward the mark of the high call in Christ Jesus..."

Philippians 3:11-13 (KJV)

"For as in one body we have many members, and the members do not all have the same func-

tion, so we, though many, are one body in Christ, and individually members one of another."

Romans 12:4-5 (ESV)

"Perseverance must finish its work so that you may be mature and complete, not lacking anything."

James 1:4 (NIV)

"Submit yourselves, then, to God. Resist the devil, and he will flee from you. Come near to God and he will come near to you."

James 4:7-8 (NIV)

SECTION THREE

THE CONTINUAL QUESTS

Affirmation

"We make a living by what we get, but we make a life by what we give."

Winston Churchill

Scripture

Now, therefore, thus says the Lord of Hosts: Consider your ways. You have sown much, and havested little. You eat, but you never have enough; you drink, but you never have your fill. You clothe yourselves, but no one is warm. And he who earns wages does so to put the into a bag with holes.

Haggai 1:5-6 (ESV)

LifeQuest™ is a journey, not a destination. For this reason, there will need to be continual maintenance required to attend to the areas of your life. Up to this point, you have to be focused on the relationships in your life and intentionally clarifying your role and responsibilities to them as well as your emotional and mental wellbeing. Your efforts have been to clear out the clutter and right the wrongs so that you can proceed through life with your attention, intentions, and actions appropriately directed toward purposeful goals.

The work that lies ahead is continued maintenance in the areas of relationships, emotional regulation, mental steadiness, and establishing the foundation for the ongoing self-care, stewardship, and accountability for what you have been entrusted within this life. This is the essence of living life well. God declared, "The thief's purpose is to steal and kill and destroy. My purpose is to give them a rich and satisfying life" (John 10:10, NLT). It is past time for us to be living out the purpose of a rich and satisfying life! This is not a declaration of just monetary wealth, but more so the prosperity of fulfillment; the fullness of joy, peace, and love; elevation about circumstances of lack and want; promotion in position and status. "Everyone to whom much was given, of him much will be required, and from him to whom they entrusted much, they will demand the more" (Luke 12:48, ESV).

I want you to imagine the skeleton of a tree or, better yet, draw it. Use a full page of paper so that you can process what I am describing and use it in your awareness. Start with a thick trunk that grows from deep roots. I envision an aged oak tree where the root structure is growing even above the ground and the canopy of limbs stretch far and wide, casting a great shadow of shade. Do you have the visual?

Now consider the root structure as the thoughts and beliefs you operate from, the trunk as the actions, behaviors, and habits that have grown from those thoughts and beliefs, and the limbs/branches are what carry the fruit that ultimately is produced. Since it is easiest to recognize the habits and behaviors, you may want to start with there.

Write all of the habits and behaviors that you are aware of in your life and consider if they are producing positive outcomes in your life. For instance, procrastination is a common habit that people live with. The thoughts or beliefs that are rooted in that habit might be "I don't have time to do that right now, I'll get to it later" or "I am going to just watch this one show, and then I'll get to work on my task." Before you know it, one show leads to another, and then another until you are no longer motivated to work on the task. The branches that grow from procrastination may be a missed deadline or an all-nighter and the stress of getting it done at the last minute. Finally, the fruit that grows from procrastination could be a lower grade or a lost account/case at work, or even reprimand or termination.

Another behavior might be poor financial management or lack of a spending plan. The thoughts and beliefs that support that behavior might be "as long as I have enough to pay the minimum balance, I can buy what I want on credit" or "I pay my bills and spend the rest on whatever I want so I don't need to write it down." This kind of thinking grows into tree limbs of debt that bear the fruit of disconnected utilities, repossessed vehicles, and a host of missed opportunities because you are unable to afford the ticket or the cost of the purchase.

I am sure there are more. Think about your "Steward

Tree" and what the costs consequences have been for your failure at being a responsible steward over the things within your control and accountability; your health, parenting your child(ren), your finances, and your time/talents/gifts. What about the lives of people who are depending on you? The last two Quests in this journey will focus on stewardship and accountability for your physical wellness because you need the container to carry you around in order for you to fulfill your purpose, and finally, your finances and other treasures that are resources for you to use in the fulfillment of your life's purpose. It will be necessary for you to be self-regulated and controlled in order for you to appropriately manage your resources and priorities appropriately. It is not a one-time feat but a continual balancing act that may require occasional recalibrations. Remember, this is a journey, not a destination. The work is not complete until the Lord returns or calls the mission complete and takes you to your heavenly destination.

Proclamation

I acknowledge that I have habits that I have acquired over the years of my life that work against my desire for good health. Some of my patterns of behavior are the result of conditioning and were the result of someone else's decision to nourish me with foods compromised by salt, sugar, and saturated fats. Now that I have information that raises my awareness about how these things and others sabotage my health, putting me at a higher risk for diseases that threaten my life, I will commit to making better decisions. I know that I am in control of what I do or do not do. I will use what I know and will seek to understand what I need to in order to make the desired improvements. Realizing that nothing is more powerful than a changed mind, I will change my mind so that my health and life will change for the better.

PHYSICAL QUEST

Affirmation

"We are creatures of habit, we often do the same things expecting a different result; break out of the old habits by doing something differnt."

Unknown

Scripture

"I praise you because I am fearfully and wonderfully made."

Psalm 139:14 (NIV)

Prayer

Lord, I come to you aware of my physical struggles. My mind knows what I need to do, but my flesh is undisciplined to carry out what I know. I surrender my excuses to you right now because the reality is that I will never have enough time in my schedule if I don't make the time. I will hurt every time I exercise if I do not stick with it long enough for my body to adjust. I have tried it in my own might; now, I am determined to stop trying and start doing. Open my eyes and ears that I may see and hear the things that will enlighten me about my health and wellbeing. Open my mind that I will understand my role in changing my behaviors in order that I will begin to contribute to my wellness instead of my illness. Lord, meet me at the point of my efforts and give just what I need to take the next step, and when I take that step, meet me there. For every action that I make, give me the confidence of what I hope for and your blessed assurance that I will have the health and fitness that I hope for even though I do not see it yet. Your Word declares, "Faith is the confidence that what we hope for will actually happen; it gives us assurance about things we cannot see" (Hebrews 11:1, NLT). I have faith in my physical health and wellness, and where my faith is weak, strengthen it and also me. I thank you for it in advance, in Jesus' name, *Amen!*

Objectives

- Review the Discovery exercises from the previous session and note the outcomes.
- To value me and my wellness enough to take ownership and responsibility for my role in establishing and maintaining physical health.
- To become aware of my family history as it relates to my personal health risks.
- To seek to learn and understand my Health Report Card and pursue information about ways to improve my outcomes.
- To stop making excuses and make an effort instead.
- To shift my focus to health and rather than weight, diet, or size, knowing that a "healthier" me may result in a change in me by size and weight!

The Physical Quest is a process of assessing your overall physical wellness. During this part of your journey, you will be challenged to consider what you do, and do not do, what you eat and do not eat, what you drink, and how much. You will also need to consider how well you take care of yourself and what habits you have established that promote physical wellness or distract from it. Do you even know what is contributing to or inhibiting you from accomplishing your divine purpose? The truth is, even when you know what the Lord has purposed you for, you may not be able to fulfill it if you are not physically capable because you are too tired, too weak, lack the stamina or strength necessary to accomplish it. Perhaps you are incapable because you are ill or limited because of a diagnosis or disease. It could even be that you are unable to do what God has purposed you to do because you are too stressed or anxious because you are carrying the responsibility of so many other things that are what you chose to do, but not what you were called to do. What is your excuse for not being physically capable of being used for God's divine purpose in your life? If you know the reason, are you willing to make some changes so that you can be physically fit?

Consider the "*choices*" you are making that inhibit or compromise your ability to be "Fit for Service." Accept the fact that you have the ability to choose behaviors that are conducive to the best quality of health and physical fitness. It may be necessary for you to determine the origin of your thoughts that influence your choices. We are all products of the environment and culture that we grew up in and were exposed to. Our environment is a powerful training ground for how we live. We actually learn what we live. Remember that what we receive, we perceive, then believe, and ultimately becomes our perspective. However, it is your prerogative to make a different decision.

I listened to a sermon by Bishop T. D. Jakes on the subject of "Change." In the message, he said, "there is nothing more powerful than a changed mind." He went on to offer the reference of a computer. When it comes from the factory, it is pre-programmed with default settings. The computer does exactly what it was pre-programmed to do. It does not mean that it cannot perform operations outside of the framework of the defaults, but in order for it to do that, the defaults have to be disabled and reprogrammed. The same is true of our minds when it comes to habits. Some things are pre-programmed from the environment we grew up in or the culture that influenced us. Some of the habits we have were established during our childhood as we consumed a diet full of high fat, cholesterol-rich, and starchy foods on a routine basis. Our pallets were conditioned early in our lives to crave sugar and salt or bread and other carbohydrates. Now that we have practiced those habits over the years of our life, some of them may have become addictions and a real struggle to overcome. It doesn't help that almost everything we purchase to eat is loaded with sugar, salt, or both in order to extend the shelf life of the pre-packaged food. Even things that would otherwise be healthy choice options are compromised because the preservatives meant to prolong their longevity likely does the opposite to our lives.

You may have noted that I am using personal pronouns in this chapter and including myself in the messaging. It is intentional because as I am writing this Quest for Life, I have been applying it in my own life for years. I am doing the work and have added many of the applications and changes that I have recommended for you to my own life. Without a doubt, the most difficult mile of my journey has been the Physical Quest. I, like you, am a product of my environment. My family of origin is from the South; my mother from Texas, father from Alabama. In my family, we cooked and ate like southerners; ham and salt pork as the meat boiled into our beans and greens; butter added to almost everything cooked, meats were often fried or smoked, and in Texas, sweet tea should have been called a dessert instead of a beverage. Don't misunderstand me, the food tasted good to me, it just was not good for me in the way it was prepared. I love and respect my grand-mothers and mother for feeding and caring for me. They did what they knew and the best they could. Thank you!

My paternal grandmother, who lives in Alabama, raises her own chickens and fresh vegetables in her garden; how-ever, if prepared with the fat and salt of traditional southern cooking, the nutritional value is severely compromised before the food arrives at the table. On my Texas family side, we ate sugar on rice and beans, the cornbread was sweet, and yams were definitely candied. I ate like they did and taught my children to eat that way because I put sugar on their food; it was the norm in my family. All of these delicacies prepared and eaten with sugar set me up for an appetite for sugar. The craving has subsequently become a stronghold for me. It is the one thing in my diet that I most struggle with getting under control. Even knowing the threat it poses to my overall health and wellness, I am significantly challenged to break the hold it has on me so that I can be healthier. It is an ongoing battle! Hypertension, high cholesterol, and diabetes are trending in my family on both sides. I am determined to overcome through Christ!

I shared my testimony with you at the beginning about being a breast cancer survivor and being twenty years cancer-free. There were so many lessons that were learned from having that diagnosis. One of the most important lessons learned is that stress is a contributory to cancer, as it is to so many other diseases that some of you may be fighting through. Hopefully, you processed the sources of your stress and the baggage you are carrying during the Emotional Quest and have made some sound decisions that will significantly reduce and ultimately balance your life in a way that is noticeably more stress-free. For me, as

I continue to do the work of LifeQuest™ in my own life, I refuse to give up or give in. I know what it takes, and I set myself up for success by keeping sweets off of my routine shopping list. I know that if I buy and have it in the house, I will eat it. That is not to say that I have mastered the cravings because I have not. I still buy the occasional treats; however, I don't usually buy the bag or full-sized items anymore. I buy single-serving sizes, feed my craving and continue to strive to keep them in balance and ultimately overcome them. Truth!

There is a scripture in Romans that states it so well. Paul is struggling with his sinful nature and says, "I don't understand myself, for I want to do what is right, but I don't do it. Instead, I do what I hate" (Romans 7:15, NLT). I know the struggle! I like you to continue my journey, doing the work that I need to do. It helps that I have a daughter who is my constant conscience. It starts with a decision, a changed mind. It does not end there. The action must follow, but a changed mind matters.

I am reminded of a woman who was in an abusive relationship. She had been in that relationship for many years by the time she decided to seek counseling. She was so emotionally wounded and financially dependent that she believed the lies he told her. Even with all that she had suffered in that marriage, she was not getting counseling because she wanted out of the relationship. Instead, she was emotionally overwhelmed over learning her husband was having an extra-marital affair, and she was afraid he would leave her for the other woman. It took some time, but when she began to receive the counsel that she is valuable and worth so much more, her perception began to shift. Finally, the day came when she considered her own worth and that of her child. When at last she believed that she deserved more, she changed her mind. When she changed her mind, her whole life was changed for the better. That woman now owns her own business, bought her own home, is putting her child through college, and enjoying her changed life!

This story may not seem like it has any relevance to physical wellbeing, but I shared it to demonstrate the power of a changed mind. Nothing happens until, first, you change your thought process. Remember the storybook character, the little engine that could? Its mantra was, I think I can, I think I can, I think I can—I did!

Remember that faith I mentioned earlier? The Bible also says, "...faith by itself, if it does not have works, is dead" (James 2:17, NKJV). That means that it is not enough to just have faith; you have to take action also. In other words, just wanting to be physically fit and praying, in faith, for God to make it so is not enough. Don't misunderstand me; God could certainly make us physically fit without any effort on our parts if He would. The reality is that His way usually requires us to do what we can do, and He will do what we cannot. Our bodies are not machines, like cars that can be traded in for a new version when it wears out. We only get one body, and it is our responsibility to maintain it in such a way that it effectively carries us through our life circumstances and continues to operate optimally to fulfill our purpose. We do have the option to ignore or mistreat our bodies and deal with the outcome. It is a choice.

When you see yourself as a Vessel, what I call the "Container of You," you should also accept that you are not the container; you are the content. However, you need the container to carry you through life. Ideally, the container will maintain good integrity and effectively perform its duty. Consider your own physical wellness, what do you need to do, what mindset needs to change for you? What will it take for you to decide that you are worth the effort, worth the time, worth *it*?

I present to you this challenge to assess your cultural influences; diet, sleep habits, tobacco use, alcohol use, consistent physical activity. Do you need to change your habits and lifestyle to ensure that you are physically fit and able to accomplish your purpose?

Make a list of things you need to do to move you from where you are and get you closer to where you want/need to be. Don't forget to include your mental health as you are seeking information about your family history. What mental health diagnosis exists in your family of origin? This is a touchy subject for many people. In some cultures, it is a forbidden topic of discussion. If you do not have anyone in your family who is able to answer your questions, for whatever reason, document your own moods, attitudes, and coping skills. Do you struggle with regulating your emotions or find that you are typically moody and have emotions that swing from one extreme to another? Are you often anxious or panicked about stressful situations? If you are aware of these things in your life and question your ability to respond to them in an appropriate way, demonstrating resilience; make a call, schedule an appointment, take some action toward accomplishing a goal that would demonstrate sound judgment.

I encourage you to know your personal health report card. Do a personal health assessment (PHA). You can start with your own knowledge and record what you know from your family history. Attention to health risk factors will guide your efforts for health promotion and disease prevention. Your primary care physician can do a full physical, order lab work and other tests that will give you a picture of your health. Finally, you can go online and search for a PHA questionnaire and complete it to learn your score and where you are currently. This information is the beginning of knowing your next steps for establishing goals for improving your overall wellbeing. Instead of being a slave to your thoughts and behaviors, be the master of them!

Reflection

Throughout this Physical Quest, you have been presented with questions about your family history, environmental and cultural influences on your behavior, and discipline or lack of discipline concerning your physical and mental wellness. At this point in your journey, use a notebook, digital note, or journal to document the collection of information that you have obtained so that it is documented in one location for your reference. This exercise will serve as your "Health Report Card," and you will be able to track your progress as you are making changes and improving your physical and mental health. You will need this baseline so that you are able to know where you started from. It is not my intention to have you focused on the number on the scale or on the tag on the neck of your garment. It is to have you focus on the numbers on your lab report; triglycerides, glucose, blood pressure, etc. Endeavor to be healthy with all of your numbers within normal range versus having a goal of weighing a certain weight or wearing a particular size. Trust me, when you are healthy and living a lifestyle conducive to maintaining good health, your weight and size will fall into range as well.

In addition to the information already mentioned, your "Health Report Card" should be dated and include your age, gender, height, and weight. Note the date of your last physical exam. A timeline for your to consider; healthy people under forty years of age should get a complete physical every four years or at the advice of your personal physician, between forty-fifty, every two years or at the advice of your personal physician, and fifty years of age and over annually or at the advice of your personal physician. Women should note their yearly mammogram (biennial age forty-fifty), depending on family history of breast cancer. Women should also note monthly menstrual cycle and self-breast exams; also pap smear (frequency as recommended by personal physician). Men should note routine prostate exam and PSA as recommended. Dental and eye exams can also be documented for reference. What is your blood type? By the way, there is a great book entitled *Eat Right For Your Type* by Dr. Peter J. D'Adamo. The book offers some noteworthy information regarding how your body processes the food you intake based on your blood type. It could be another helpful resource for you.

Proclamation

I proclaim that you have begun a good work in me, my Lord, and I know that you are faithful to see it through to completion. I, too, will carry on with this work that I am doing unto your service and will devote myself to continuing it until you say, "Well done, good and faithful servant, now come and take your rest!"

FINANCIAL QUEST

Affirmation

"We make a living by what we get, but we make a life by what we give. "

Winston Churchill

Scriptures

"...From everyone who has been given much, much will be demanded; and from the one who has been entrusted with much, much more will be asked."

Luke 12:48b (NIV)

"By the Holy Spirit who dwells within us, guard the good deposit entrusted to you."

2 Timothy 1:14 (ESV)

Prayer

Lord, Thank you for all that you have entrusted to me. As I embark on this mile of the journey, help me to consider what I am accountable for in my life. Show me where I need to adjust my behaviors in order to be a better steward of the gifts, talents, skills, resources, and lives you have given me responsibility for. I also desire to manage myself in a way that is disciplined and respectful of the time I have in a twenty-four-hour day. Help me not waste time or opportunities to appropriately use what you have given me to effectively serve, minister to, or impact the lives of the people you place in my life. Finally, the life you have given me has a limited amount of time on this earth to carry out the purpose for which you allowed me to be here. Don't let me waste it chasing selfish intentions and meaningless objectives. May this life be used to advance your Kingdom and being a blessing to others. I seek your approval more than the praise of mankind. Help me to do your will. Amen.

Objectives

- Review the *discovery* exercises from the previous session and note the outcomes.
- Learn the meaning of Stewardship and what it means for your life journey.
- Discover the things in my life that I am Accountable to God for.
- Raise Awareness about your "Circle of Priorities."
- Balance.

This process is about stewardship and accountability for your many resources, including time, treasures, talents, skills, and other things that the *Lord* has given you responsibility for. This is about you demonstrating and exercising responsibility as a part of humankind in the greater society, as a parent of the child(ren) you conceived and the ones that were bonuses, as a business owner, or staff as part of someone else's business. This is another reminder that "to whom much is given, much will be required" (Luke 12:48, KJV). This is a lifelong charge that we have been given; however, we all tend to shift our focus onto things that are only superficial, and we lose sight of what matters most. I entitled this mile of the journey the Financial Quest, but it is not just about money. Money is simply a resource. It is necessary to have money to accomplish some things, but it is not the source, and it is not what matters most. I used this term because it stands for wealth, an abundance of valuable possessions, a plentiful supply of a particular resource, according to Google's English Dictionary.

There is a saying, "money cannot buy happiness." The person who said that was likely very financially sovereign and not accustomed to having a lack or want. On the other hand, a person who does not have enough money would likely disagree and would certainly welcome an opportunity to prove the theory wrong. I would wager that it would not be long before that person would agree. Once the person had been given enough time to deal with all of the issues that come with riches; the eventual demands of family and friends for loans or outright monetary grants, and after s/he has splurged on enough material things and eventually realizes that the next car is just another car, the next house is just another house, another handbag, pair of shoes, etc., and you can only drive or wear one at a time; having riches will become less meaningful. I know there are those exceptions that are the outliers. Some of the richest people are also some of the most lonely and unhappy ones. A person who has an abundance of money, but is still unhappy because s/he does not have an authentic, loving relationship, is under constant pressure to perform, or any number of other things that money cannot solve has a totally different perspective about money. If you make it your source, it will dictate how you live, and the quality of your life will be determined by how much or how little you have. "Do not lay up for yourselves treasures on earth, where moth and rust destroy and where thieves break in and steal; but lay up for yourselves treasures in heaven, where neither moth nor rust destroys and where thieves do not break in and steal. For where your treasure is, there your heart will be also" (Matthew 6:19-21, NJKV).

Seen as a resource, you will be less likely to hoard it selfishly and more willing to use it selflessly for whatever God directs you to. You may be more sensitive to the needs in the lives of others around you that you could use the resource of money to fulfill. It is about the relationship you have with your finances that will determine if you are a good steward, if you are managing it, or if it is controlling you. Financial management and accountability are learned behaviors, and anything that is learned can also be adjusted by learning and developing new habits and behaviors.

People often talk about "time management" as if we have control over time. Well, I am sorry to disappoint you, but we do not have control over time; it is a twenty-four-hour continuum and is not controlled by any man, not even through the man-made concept of daylight savings time.

What you control or manage is how you utilize the time that we exist within. I like to call it a "circle of priorities." Every day, the clock starts over, and you have a "new" twenty-four-hour "circle of priorities." You determine how you will spend that twenty-four-hour span of time and how you will prioritize how much the tasks and people get of it. You do not get to carry over any time from the day before, and you do not get to extend the day you are currently in, so when the twenty-four hours expire, you start another day and another "circle of priorities." This is no easy feat, especially for people who have a spouse and child(ren) making demands at that time. Add to that other family and loved ones who also make demands for their fair share. This becomes even more complicated if the child has special needs or if you are responsible for aging parents or someone requiring additional care because of their own limited abilities. We have not even begun to calculate the myriad of other priorities such as work, school, and extra-curricular activities. It does not stop there because I have not listed the most critical of priorities; spiritual growth and nurturance, your own physical and mental self-care, and social outlets; oh and *sleep*. How do you get it all in?

When I speak to small and large audiences, I like to use various techniques to appeal to the different learning styles; Visual, Auditory, and Kinesthetic. For the visual learner, imagine you have a plate, and you begin to place balls labeled with each of your responsibilities onto the plate. Continue to pile the balls on top of each other until the capacity of the plate prohibits you from successfully adding without a ball falling off. It's a no-brainer to realize that the capacity of the plate is limited, and eventually, balls are going to begin to fall off. The ah-ha moment is when you read the label on the balls that fall off and realize it's your marriage, or your child(ren), or your health. The impact begins to sink in at that point because the reality is you are just piling it on with no thought to the fact that you may not be able to control what falls.

The relationship with your spouse is broken because it was not in your "circle of priorities" or did not get enough of your time and resulted in a divorce, and now you have to figure out how you will fit in time to balance the shared parenting time that was written into the divorce agreement. What about the relationship with the child(ren) that is broken because it was not given enough time on your "circle of priorities"? It resulted in the need to add trips to the therapist or to the probation or parole officer to your schedule because that relational priority was out of balance. This is not a theory; it is a reality in far too many lives. For me, it was my physical health that fell out of balance. I ate what was convenient more than what was healthy. I cared for the wellness of others more than myself; I carried the weight of burdens that belonged to others or to the Lord instead of allowing their issues to be their own and turning over the heavy burdens to the Lord and not trying to carry them myself. This is not just a story that I am telling you, it is real life, and it is a journey that is navigated every day by each and every one of us.

The continuation of this journey requires balance, order, and discipline. The formula is written in our instruction book for life, The Holy Bible. I like to see this as an acronym "His Official Language Your Basic Instructions Before Leaving Earth." You are instructed to "Seek Him in all you do, and He will show you which path to take" (Proverbs 3:6, NLT). Start there. Each day should begin and end with a conversation with God where you are seeking him for the direction of your day and the coordinates that will balance the priorities you have with the amount of time you have.

The next thing is to get some order to your life; a plan. The Lord said, "Write my answer plainly on tablets so that a runner can carry the correct message to others" (Habakkuk 2:2, NLT). Writing things down will help you to have a plan and some accountability for how you manage yourself within the time you have. Establishing a daily schedule, putting things on a calendar, pre-planning menus, shopping lists, spending plans, etc., are all ways of writing out the plan for each day so that you can set yourself up for success. And one step further might be to set a clock alarm to prompt you when you need to move on to the next thing. Having this kind of order in your life will help you to ensure that you are intentional about making time for your marriage, your child(ren), your parents, yourself, and the many other things that are in your "circle of priorities." Sometimes quality time is more meaningful than the quantity of time.

I have about an hour and ten minutes one-way commute each weekday to and from work. One way I maximized my time is I use that time in the car for a variety of multiple tasks, i.e., conversations with mom, sister, daughters, and others. I sometimes use it for self-care, and I listen to an audiobook that ministers to me spiritually, mentally, or emotionally. Other times, it is used for quiet self-reflective thought that resets my mind and prepares me to come home to my husband in a better state of mind with a more pleasant disposition.

Make a list of your current priorities: "Spiritual Growth," "Relationships," "Career/School," "Physical Health," "Mental/Emotional Wellness," "Self-Care," "Social Outlets," "Sleep/Rest," "Chores/Tasks," and "Preparations/Transitions."

There are some absolutes that are essential to life balance. The first is that sleep is absolutely essential to balance and harmony in your life. The caveat is that we do not all require the same amount of sleep in order to realize the balance needed. In order to truly know the optimum amount of sleep you need personally, it would be helpful to know your circadian rhythm; your natural synchronization with time. When it is possible, operating within that rhythm will provide the most natural life cycle and flow of daily functioning. Unfortunately, most of us are forced by our circumstances to operate on the rhythm that aligns with our work schedule or life schedule with tasks and responsibilities. Those of you who are functioning on a different schedule because you have a newborn who wakes for feedings every two to three hours can relate to what I am saying. I was born in the midnight/early morning hours and am very much a nocturnal creature. When I am allowed to follow my natural rhythm, I am able to think and produce best in the late night and earliest morning hours. However, because I work in a profession and career that requires me to work on a more traditional schedule, I have to adjust and alter my sleep cycle. Ideally, seven-eight hours of sleep is what is needed to give my mind and body their optimum amount of rest. On a typical day, when I am doing my best scheduling and preparing for a normal workday, I should be in bed by 10:00 p.m. because I have to be at work by 8 a.m., and I have to factor in about three hours of preparations and transitions. Preparations and transitions are also essential. Preparations are the time needed to get showered, dressed, makeup on, breakfast, lunch, and bag packed. Transitions are the time it takes to get from place to place of from one priority to the next, i.e., the commute/drive to and from work (over an hour each way on a good day for me). When I have not planned well, time has to be taken from other priorities in my circle.

Each person's priorities may be different, and the amount of time needed will also vary from person to person. Depending on your stage in life, you may be a student seeking a degree and working at a full-time career. On the other hand, you may be retired and no longer required to go to work or school. You may personally choose to live in smaller or less desirable accommodations because you value your time for other priorities over long drives or commutes. Each situation and personal values are different.

Consider your own situation. Think about the optimum amount of sleep you need and the time you have to get up in the morning in order to start your day. Count backward that amount of sleep hours to get your target bedtime. Everything else is about planning the events of the day and fitting them into the remaining hours in your twenty-four-hour "circle of priorities." On the days when you have more priorities than time, something has to be adjusted.

It is a balancing act. Some days career/school gets more time, and relationships are deferred. Other days relationships make it to the list, and self-care gets put off. Some days you may even get a two or three-fer, a spa day, and lunch with a good friend that counts for self-care, relationship, and possibly emotional wellness! The key is to have balance and to not neglect any one thing for too long. Otherwise, balance is lost, and something falls and possibly breaks. What good is it to have worked so long and hard for that successful job, degree, promotion, award, etc., only to lose the family you wanted to share it with?

It is critical that you always fit in spiritual growth. Likewise, preparing ahead of time could actually save you time in the long run. And finally, everyone will have transitions which can sometimes be wasted time if not well managed—for instance, sitting at the car dealership while your task of getting the oil changed is wasted time if you fail to use that time to do something else in your "circle of priorities." That is a great time to work on your shopping list or listen to a good book (self-care) or plan your schedule for the next day or week (preparation). You could even drop the car off and call that a transition while you go on to do something else on your "circle of priorities." It's your time, a valuable resource; be a good steward of it.

I am reminded of the parable of the talents in Matthew 25:14-30,

A master who was leaving his house to travel, and, before leaving entrusted his property to his servants. To one he gave five talents, to another two, to another one. To each he gave according to their level of ability. When he returned, he discovered that the one who received five had doubled what he was given, as had the one with two. But the one that only received one talent chose to bury it and do nothing out of fear so the master took back the one talent and gave it to the one who now had ten.

God expects us to be faithful stewards over what He gives us, and He will reward our faithfulness. As you manage your small circle of priorities in your life well, He will notice and say, "well done, my good and faithful servant," and promote you in the business of the Kingdom. Your life and others depend on it.

Resolve

As I look around at the state of my society and greater community, I realize that there are some who are dealing with lack and want when others have plenty by comparison. I am aware that what I have is a result of your love and kindness more than my entitlement. Thank you! Help me to show my appreciation for what I have by taking care of it and utilizing it for the purpose for which it is intended. I want to be a cheerful giver; I want to recognize the needs of others and respond with selfless benevolence. I want to give an account to you for my life and all that you have entrusted to me in life, without guilt or shame. I want to bless every life and situation that you intend me to. I realize that you have great expectations of me in my life because you have given me much. I hear the call and accept the assignment. I will do what you have purposed and equipped me to do for the sake of the Kingdom. I will grow what you have entrusted me with and will be that good and faithful servant. It is my reasonable service!

SECTION FOUR

SECTION FOUR

LiViNG THE QUEST

Affirmation

"Your Stewardship has the potential to influence lives, provide hope to others, and make an eternal difference."

Unknown

Scripture

"Commit to the Lord whatever you do, and He will establish your plans."

Proverbs 16:3 (NIV)

Prayer

Lord, I am committed to the ongoing LifeQuest™ journey. I will use the resources available to me to prepare for the balance, order, and plans for my life's work by doing a *vision board* that will serve as a visual reference for my goals and will remind me often of where my focus and efforts should be. I will be prayerful and thoughtful as I consider my goals each year, and I will surrender to you, procrastination, and every other stronghold that would seek to distract or derail me from accomplishing the goals laid out before me. I will look for the help that you have made available to support, encourage and hold me accountable in this process, and most of all, I will *trust you* in the process. *Amen*, and it is so.

Objectives

- Review the *discovery* exercises from the previous session and note the outcomes.
- Use the revelations and discoveries of all of the Quests to help me grow and progress in my journey.
- To connect all of the lessons learned throughout the journey of LifeQuest and determine visual references for accountability and apply them to specific goals
- Create a three-dimensional or virtual/digital Vision Board.
- Reference your Vision Board at least three times per week.

Now that you have all of the milestones for each of the Quests, continue living your quest of life by creating a visual reference (vision board) with at least one goal for each of the seven quests. The vision board should be creative and representative of your individual style and personality. This is a personal dashboard for your goals and forward progression in your journey. Vision Boards can be digital or three-dimensional and should include images and words. It should be organized in a thematic way. Your *Vision Board* should be considered a living reference that evolves with the goals and accomplishments in your life. It should be put in a place of relevance where you are able to see it daily. The *Vision Board* should be reviewed and refreshed at least *yearly*.

Reflections

Identify at least one SMART goal for each of the seven quests:

Spiritual_____

_____

Sexual _____

_____

Social _____

_____

Emotional _____

_____

Mental _____

_____

Physical _____

_____

Financial _____

_____

Transfer the identified goals to the vision board with a relevant image and/or words that will trigger your thoughts and actions to strive toward achievement of the goals.

Resolve

I have embarked upon this journey in pursuit of my God-given divine purpose. I have accepted the call and discovered that in doing so, I have the Holy Spirit walking right alongside me. He has revealed many discoveries along the way; some I knew but did not realize the significance, others I was completely unaware of. However, now that I know, I can deal with what I know and use what I have learned for my own life improvements and share with others that they also may overcome. I recognize that God has uniquely created me and equipped me with particular gifts, talents, and skillsets. He did it on purpose so that I could accomplish what He desires me to do while on this earth—wow, what a loving Father! I will no longer question, wonder, or doubt that I am *whole*, nothing missing or lacking. I have everything I need, and I will use what I have been given as it was intended; a good steward. I know that the day will come when I will stand before my creator and give account for all that I was given and what I did with it. I want to stand humbled but proud when I report that I did just what you said with what you gave me, Lord. I did not bury it, but I multiplied it and used it to advance the Kingdom of God. I want to hear you say, "Well done, good and faithful servant. You have been faithful over a little; I will set you over much. Enter into the joy of your Master" (Matthew 25:21, ESV).

I will continue this journey, following your lead, until you come for me!

AFTERWORD

LifeQuest™ may have placed some spiritual, emotional, mental, and physical demands on you as a reader. It is easy to breeze through the reading without doing the work, but if you accepted the challenge and committed to do the self-introspective work, you were sure to discover some needs for change. We all have issues with people or how we are doing in life that could use some fine-tuning. Hopefully this journey has challenged your existing philosophies for your life and prompted you to make changes and adaptation. If you have not already done so, begin now to considering your story (testimony). The one where God delivered you through a diagnosis, loss, victimization, hurt. Something that broke your heart or shaped your heart to be compassionate toward a certain group of people is likely the essence of your story. Begin to record the details of your story.

I encourage you to seek professional help if old wounds have been opened or new hurts have been caused by this LifeQuest™ experience. You should have made note of some professionals in your area when working through the Emotional Quest, but if you did not, contact your local crisis center to seek assistance. I have added a Suggested Reading List of some of my preferred reads.

SUGGESTED READING FOR PERSONAL GROWTH

Relational Quests (Spiritual, Sexual, Social)

The Five Love Languages by Dr. Gary Chapman

His Needs, Her Needs by Willard F. Harley Jr.

Love and Respect by Dr. Emerson Eggerichs

Every Woman's Battle by Shannon Ethridge

Every Man's Battle by Stephen Arterbun and Fred Stoeker

Wild at Heart by John Eldredge

Captivating by John Eldredge & Stasi Eldredge

Faith is Not a Feeling by Ney Bailey

The Prayer that Changes Everything by Stormie Omartian

Your Best Life Now by Joel Osteen

How to Hear From God by Joyce Meyer

Lord Disciple Me by Richard Mull

Lord Heal Me by Richard Mull

The Last Lecture by Randy Pausch

The Truth About Cheating by Gary Neuman

Love Worth Giving by Max Lucado

Alone Together by Dr. Albright

Confident Woman by Joyce Meyer

So You Call Yourself a Man by T. D. Jakes

HeMotions by T. D. Jakes

Generational Imperative by Chuck Underwood

Jesus by Beth Moore

The Shack by William P. Young

Crazy Good Sex: Putting to Bed the Myths Men Have About Sex by Les Parrott

When God Intervenes by Dabney Hedegard

The Necessary Nine: How to Stay Happily Married for Life by Dan Seaborn and Peter Newhouse, PhD.

Continual Quests

Self-improvement

LifeQuest: The Journey Through The Maze of Life by Dr. Dora B. Mays

Battlefield of the Mind: Winning the Battle in Your Mind by Joyce Meyer

A Love Worth Giving by Max Lucado

My Stroke of Insight by Dr. Jill Bolte

The Wounded Heart: Hope for Adult Victims of Childhood Sexual Abuse by Dr. Dan Allender

Fearless by Max Lucado

Quiet Strength by Tony Dungy

UnCommon by Tony Dungy

Boundaries by Dr. Henry Cloud and Dr. John Townsend

The Bondage Breaker by Neil T. Anderson

Necessary Endings by Henry Cloud

Breaking Free by Beth Moore

Molecules of Emotions by Candice Pert

Facing the Giants by Max Lucado

Let It Go by T. D. Jakes

The Resilience Factor by Karen Reivich and Andrew Shatte

Flourish by Martin E. P. Seligman

Authentic Happiness by Martin E. P. Seligman

The Power of Resilience by Robert Brooks and Sam Goldstein

Change Your Words, Change Your Life by Joyce Meyer

CPSIA information can be obtained
at www.ICGtesting.com
Printed in the USA
BVHW041518161121
621776BV00015B/528

9 781637 693483